History of Lexington Township

Including Alliance, Limaville, and Mt. Union

By Levi L. Lamborn

Alliance Historical Society

Alliance, Ohio

CONTENTS

Dr. Levi L. Lamborn

Foreword

LAMBORN'S NOTES[1]

No correction of errors of typography or grammar will be attempted, which may occur in the chapters of the history of Lexington Township; but all additional facts or errors of date, or feature of facts that can be learned, as having occurred in preceding chapters will be rectified and added in foot notes to subsequent chapters. Scrutiny is solicited upon these points. The recollection of a party from whom information is obtained may be uncertain as regards a date, which another person not personally seen is positive about. So with certain phases and additional features of facts, any information bearing upon the history of the township left orally or in writing with the Editor of the *Local* will be thankfully received, credited and appropriated.

---

[1] Originally published as ERRATA ET ADDENDA to the February 1, 1873 article

TRANSCRIBER'S NOTES

Having reviewed the written records of the history of the Alliance community for several years now, I have discovered that much of this history is based on the Business Directory published by Stuart McKee in 1868, and these articles published in the *Alliance Weekly Local* in 1873. Levi Lamborn had lived in this area for almost forty years, serving as a physician, newspaper publisher, real estate developer, banker and horticulturist. This is the earliest cataloguing of historical facts for the Alliance community.

As with many histories of the second part of the 19th century, some care is necessary in interpreting the facts as presented here. Lamborn makes clear he was attempting an accurate depiction of the previous seventy years, however, it is worth remembering that he was also keenly interested in promoting the fortunes of the Alliance community because of his real estate holdings. Also common to histories of the time is a romantic nostalgia for the "pioneer days," and the people who lived in those times. It is probably akin to our current (c. 2004) feelings about "The Greatest Generation" and their "Good War" (World War II). Additionally, there are several letters published within the series that are first-hand accounts of events, as well as stories from early settlers told directly to Lamborn. Overall, I believe the reader will discover in these articles a sincerity and sense of humor that reassures us that this was a hearty labor of love for Lamborn.

I have attempted to faithfully transfer the typeset text as it appeared in 1873. As such, punctuation, quotation marks, italicized words, spellings and misspellings appear as they did in the newspaper. The two significant exceptions are the replacement of "e&." with the modern "etc.," and the representation of dollar amounts with commas and decimal points in our current standard. The reader may also note some obvious inaccuracies.

Robb Hyde – November 2004

EDITOR'S NOTES

It has been some time since Robb Hyde first transcribed these articles from the microfilm copies of the *Alliance Weekly Local* and since that time, changes in how to prepare this book for publication have also occurred.

In talking with Robb, we decided to publish the work in a more organized fashion, pulling like topics together and combining articles that spread across several weeks of newspapers. To preserve the historical value of the text, the original date of publication for each chapter has been noted in a footnote. A chart outlining the original chapter numbering and topics of each chapter has been supplied by Michelle Dillon.

Typographical errors have been corrected and every attempt has been made to spell out the names of individuals where abbreviations were originally used. The difference between Mt. Union, the village, and Mount Union, the college, has also been implemented to alleviate any confusion between the two entities.

All in all, we hope that this volume is now in a more logical and readable format and will serve as a reference book for those investigating Lexington Township, Alliance, and Mt. Union, from their beginnings to 1873.

Karen Perone, Alliance Historical Society
January 2018

PUBLISHING SEQUENCE AND CHAPTER HEADINGS OF LAMBORN'S HISTORY -- 1873

Lamborn, Levi L. [L.L.L.] "History of Lexington Township," as published in the *Alliance Weekly Local* (J. W. Gillespie, publisher), Saturdays between January 11 (no. 3) and September 5 (no. 37) inclusive, 1873.

Order	Chapter	Notes	Date	Page	First Line	Topic
1	I		Jan. 11	3	Some eighteen years ago	Beginning of villages
2	II		Jan. 18	3	It seems singular	Mahoning River, Lexington
3	II	dup #	Jan. 25	3	In the war between England	Indians, wild game, Isaac Teeters
4	IV		Feb. 1	3	The great snow of 1817	Wildlife, errata et addenda
5	V		Feb. 8	3	Squirrels were not so plenty	Squirrels, wolves, Hubbards, salt
6	VI		Feb. 15	3	The next great move	Grist mills and sawmills
7	VII		Feb. 22	3	The town of Lexington	Lexington, Freedom, Post office
8	VIII		Mar. 1	3	A colony of colored people	New Guinea, cabins, woolen mills
9	IX		Mar. 8	3	There is nothing so well	Pioneers, Ellis Johnson family
10	X		Mar. 15	3	The differences being so	Story of lost Pound children
11	XI		Mar. 22	3	The Lexington side of Mt.	Mt. Union, nicknames, misc.

12	XII		Mar. 29	3	Among the early settlers	Grants, J. Grant letters, addenda
13	XIII		Apr. 5	3	The first school ever opened	Schools, Mount Union College
14	XIV		Apr. 12	1	In early times, from 1806	Public lands, taxation
		none	Apr. 19			
15	XV		Apr. 26	2	On Thursday, June 8, 1854	Newspapers
16	XV	dup #	Apr. 26	4	John Shreve died at Mt.	John Shreve, Rev. war service
		none	May 3			
17	XVII		May 10	2	In 1830 the people of	Military participation, misc.
18	XVIII		May 10	4	Last week's chapter	Military persons, fruits & nuts
19	XIX	.	May 17	4	It is believed that	Berries, wheat, C. Grant letter
20	XX		May 24	3	For the following list of	Justices of the Peace
21	XXI		May 31	1	Levi Burden was the father	Justices cont'd, Alliance, Freedom
22	XXI	dup #	June 7	1	For the interest many	Dr. Day's letter, Limaville
		none	June 14			
23	XXII		June 21	2	In 1835 I purchased of Peter	Dr. Day's letter cont'd, epidemics
24	XXIII		June 28	2	In 1853 typhoid fever	Dr. Day's letter end, misc.

25	XXIV		July 5	2	Alliance is built at the	Crossing, railroads
26	XXV		July 12	2	The labors of the agent at	Railroads, hotels, Sourbeck
27	XXVI		July 19	2	As nearly as can now be	Methodist churches
28	XXVII		July 26	2	Much the same that	Addns. to Alliance, Limaville, Mt. U
29	XXVIII		Aug. 2	2	The present city government	Alliance city officials, mayors, $
30	XXIX		Aug. 9	2	On the 25th of August, 1827	Canals, RRs, Dr. Day's ghost story
31	XXX		Aug. 16	2	The history of Grape culture	Grape culture
32	XXXII	no XXXI	Aug. 16	4	The first effort made to build	Lutheran churches
		none	Aug. 23			
33	XXXIII		Aug. 30	2	In the year 1847 Levi Borton	Disciples, Baptist churches
34	XXXIV		Sept. 5	2	In the year 1857 the Disciples	Disciples, Christian church

Introduction[2]

Some eighteen years ago[3], the writer purchased in Ravenna, Ohio, a printing press and the necessary material to equip a small office, and bringing them to Alliance issued the first paper printed in the township, bearing the name of the *Alliance Ledger*.

The town then could boast of but a few hundred inhabitants, including Williamsport and Freedom; and the local patronage to a paper was of necessity very limited, and in order to create an interest in the enterprise, and augment the circulation of the *Ledger*, the idea was conceived to write up the history of the township. The design was carried out, installments of which appeared in the paper as our circumstance offered opportunity to gather up the facts.

This was considered quite a success, when nine persons out of every ten averaged that no energy or talent could rescue the effort from failure in a locality so anti-metropolitan as Alliance

---

[2] Originally published January 11, 1873

[3] 1855

was at that date. At that time, eighteen years ago, the first settlers of 1807-1808 were trembling in feebleness and age in the threshold of that home, which fast bolts its treasury of early remembrances from the prying scrutiny of enquiring posterity. But one man, resident at the above date, yet tarries with us, the rest are all gone. There are several yet in the township whose memory runs back to a decade later than the period of its first settlement.

The chronological increase of agricultural products, wealth, population of the township, etc., are garnered matters of record, open to research and examination, now as in the future.

But the arduous labors, interesting hunting exploits, depredations, heroic fortitude, reminiscences of the Indians, etc., of the pioneers of the township have their record only in the fading memories which gleam dimly on the incidents of early life.

It is the design to incorporate as much of this class of material in the subsequent chapters as has been or as can be reliably obtained.

There are many who sleep in the small, neglected, and almost forgotten graveyards of the townships, whose heirloom was heroism but whose wager of life was hard. They battled with interminable forests, wild beast, and wilder men; and today they sleep forgotten.

Their hard earned patrimony is in the fertile fields, early life, happy homes clustering in the peace and comfort—a realized legacy today. For those bequeathments we will read and write their names anew.

Early Days

FOUNDING OF LEXINGTON TOWNSHIP[4]

Settlement in Lexington Township was made in 1805-1806, by families attached to the Quaker faith, among the first of them was Amos Holloway, Zacheus Stanton, Nathan Gaskill, John Grant, David Berry and Jesse Felts. Amos Holloway emigrated from Loudoun County, Virginia, and entered the land that was chosen for the site of the village of Lexington, and in conjunction with Nathan Gaskill, was the proprietor.

The first roads laid out in this township, were the ones leading from Deerfield to Canton, diagonally across the township, and the other was from Salem, intersecting the first at the village of Lexington.

---

[4] Originally published January 11 & 18, 1873

The first post office was on the first of these routes, located in 1811, three-quarters of a mile west of the town, at the house of the pioneer, Jesse Felts. The farm is still occupied by his son, Shadrach, who had the control of the office near twelve years. A weekly mail arrived at the station. It was first carried on horseback by Judeth Farnam. It was considered an extraordinary trip to reach Canton from Deerfield in one day. The same post office, kept till it was lived down in Lexington, by Mr. William Kingsbury, a volunteer soldier in the last war with England, and who was in the reception of a pension from the government for over thirty years. In an engagement with the British on our northern frontier, he was struck with an ounce lead ball in the occipital region of the head, which deeply embedded itself and was not dislodged by surgical skill until some weeks after the accident. The old hero kept the ball and his bloody shirt till his death, which occurred in 1835, as trophies of the danger he encountered through his youthful

Plat of Lexington, 1807

patriotism. His son, Guy Kingsbury (deceased), represented the county from this township in the lower branch of the legislature, in the year 1833.[5]

Mr. Guy Kingsbury was the only resident of the township that ever represented the county in the legislature, except the Hon. Humphrey Hoover (deceased), who was elected in 1860, and re-elected in 1862. John Kingsbury, a resident of this city, was a brother to Guy Kingsbury.

The *Ohio Repository*, which was published in Canton for more than fifty consecutive years, by the respected pioneer editor, John Saxton, was the first paper received at the first office and read by the first settlers of Lexington Township.

It seems singular to the third generation that the prospecting settlers of Stark County should prefer to pitch their tents on the thin, cold, clay soil common to the immediate vicinity of Lexington, when much more fertile localities lay in close proximity. The barrens, or that section surrounding Canton, now grown, was considered, in 1806, worthless land.

Time has proven it to be the richest land in the county and peculiarly adapted to the cultivation of wheat. But there are many influences at work controlling the judgment of locating pioneers; soil and timber kindred to the kind from whence they came is not the least potential. The Mahoning at this date

---

[5] Guy Kingsbury represented this county from Lexington Township, in the Legislature in the year 1843, and died while he was a member. His widow lives on Main Street, Alliance, a well preserved and estimable old lady. One of their sons is publisher and editor of the Newark, Licking Co., *Democratic* paper. Another son lost a limb from an accident on the railroad. It was common for the volunteer soldiers of the War of 1812 to have their mess pans made the shape of their heads and wear them under their caps. The pan and shirt worn and the ball extracted from the body of William Kingsbury are now relics in the possession of his son John, a resident of this city. The Kingsbury family immigrated to this township in 1836, from the state of Vermont. – Lamborn, February 1, 1873

was a mighty river, often sweeping to the brow of its secondary embankments, its tributaries yielding it their ever constant supplies drawn from the humid soil, evaporation shut out by dense over-arching forests. It is now shorn of its majesty, and dry seasons see it dwarfed to a rivulet. Then the white-barked cottonwood trees, a few which remain along its course, though prostrated had no power to dam its waters or stay its course; they were swept as feathers from its channel.

The early settlers were of the opinion that the Mahoning was navigable and would be the highway of commerce from the Ohio River to Lexington. This opinion had much to do with the first settlers locating upon its banks and calling that location Lexington in 1805.

This stream which once was deservedly dignified by the title "river" enters the township on the southern third of its eastern border, runs a circuitous direction and passes out at its northeastern corner. At the time of the first settlement, it was well stocked with fine fish; from its waters the pioneers and Indians drew a supply of food of this kind, equal to all their wants.

Notwithstanding its present diminished volume, and interrupted waters, many good sized fish (Bass) are yet annually caught. The banks of this stream in this township, for sixty-eight consecutive years, has had its continuous line of Daniel Waltons.

The most prominent amateurs, as well as experts, at the present time, in inveighing the finny tribe to their ruin on the baited delusion, are our worthy and genial townsman, Messrs. Ridgeway Haines and James Shirtz.

Contemporary with the settlement made in Lexington Township, one was made at Kendal, now a northern ward of the city of Massillon, and probably here and there a "squatter" in two or three sections of the county.

It gives the mind a better conception of the wild and chaotic condition of things in that territory six miles square, known as Lexington Township, at the time of its first settlement, viz., 1805, to know that the County of Stark was not organized for four years after this date (1809) and the township did not possess a municipal organization for eleven years after this time, 1816.

The first house in the Town of Lexington and the first with a shingle roof in the township, was built in 1808, by Amos Holloway. In this building the first store was opened, by Gideon Hughes. The heaviest of any one article, as well as the one in which most capital was invested, was earthen-ware. This mercantile enterprise proving anti-lucrative, was soon abandoned, and this shingle-roofed St. Paul's of Lexington was used as the first house of the assemblage of public worship by the Society of Friends, and in the interim of its religious occupation, was hallowed to the noble use of "teaching the young idea how to shoot." The first pedagogue in this school was Daniel Votaw. This was a subscription school and conducted in harmony with the views of the Friends.

The land of Lexington Township was entered at two dollars per acre, and payable in three installments at the Land Office in Steubenville. In the reduction of the price of Government Land to one dollar and a quarter per acre, there was a clause permitting all who had forfeited their land by not paying the second and third installments, to re-enter Government Land at the rate of one dollar and twenty-five cents per acre, to the amount of the money they had paid on their forfeited estates.

From the scarcity of post-routes and consequent difficulty of disseminating a knowledge of enacted laws, as well as other news, in these times; the early settlers were generally ignorant of this providing clause in the new land-law; and thought they had lost all under the provision of the old law. A few men, or rascals, acquainted with the facts in the case, purchased the entry papers of numerous defaulting early settlers, for a few dollars, and paid the balance due or entered new lands to the amount that had been paid upon what had been deemed forfeited patents. The beginning of some of the largest fortunes in this section were laid by dealing in these papers. The morality of the procedure may be a question upon which the posterity of a defrauded ancestor, well known in this section of Ohio, obtained a beginning in this way, and died a couple of years ago worth one million and a half dollars.

INDIANS[6]

In the war between England and America in 1812, the British government sought in the savages, numerous in the west, and in front of the advancing tide of Caucasian civilization, emissaries to assist in the dominancy of their arms.

Prior to this period the Indians of Lexington Township were numerous. The red men throng and linger where game abounds. The forests here were alive with game, and the waters of the river filled with fish.

From the earliest settlement of the township until the war, the conduct of the Indians towards the white settlers was pacific if not kind. This to an extent is preferable to the fact that the first whites were disciples of William Penn, and the kind peaceable disposition of the members of the tribe inhabiting the

---

[6] Originally published January 25, 1873

township. We have no savage brutality upon their part, occurring in the township, to record. One white man was shot, the ball passing through both eyes and the bridge of the nose, yet lived deprived of sight. His name was Daniel Diver. He died in Deerfield in 1850, where the shooting occurred. It sprang out of a horse trade.

The Indians trapped game on the Mahoning, Beech Creek, and Deer Creek, all larger streams than now, but they had no permanent settlement in the township. Another feature which attracted the Indians to Lexington Township, beside the abundance of game was the large, compact groves of sugar trees peculiar to this township, from which they obtained a supply of the saccharine element. Some of the trees yet show the scarifications and girdlings adopted by them to obtain the water. It was also the current belief among the people of the township, even as late as 1840, that the Indians obtained their supply of lead from this immediate vicinity.

At the time of the first white settlers the Indians possessed many of the common implements incident to frontier civilization, such as guns, hatchets, axes, kettles, etc.

The chief encampment of the tribe found in this township was four miles south of New Philadelphia, in what was then Coshocton County. But it was common for Indians to stay over the hunting season, committing no depredation, and were kind and deferential to the whites.

The exact spot of one of their primitive mills is a little south of Mr. Haines' orchard. The machinery consisted of a stump hollowed out and a sapling bent over; to the pendant extremity of which was attached by throngs of tough bark a large stone, which by bearing on the bent sapling played upon the maze in the concavity of the stump, which would reduce it rapidly and effectively.

Suspicion is a strong latent or developed trait in Indian character. They raised the war whoop against the settlers in 1813. Some few settlers of the township left through fear, for more populous and better protected localities, but Commodore Perry put an effectual quietus upon the unnatural and barbarous coalition formed by England against America and the Indians, left unsupported by British gold, rum, and influence, grew sullen and suspicious — stopped all intercourse with the whites of the township, and withdrew to unoccupied, or new hunting grounds.

After 1813, only a traveling or passing Indian was seen in the township. Occasionally an Indian grave is by accident opened, revealing only some rude device for hunting less perishable than their bones — flint, darts, and stone axes, being now and then turned up by the plowman. These, with the traditions we have recorded, are the only reminders that they ever trod the soil of the township. Let them go from other places as from here, their destruction is fixed and necessary everywhere; we have no sentiment to waste on a savage.

ANIMALS IN THE AREA[7]

Wild game, at the settlement of Lexington Township, was very plenty; with the exception of beaver, which being very scarce at first, soon entirely disappeared. Otters and muskrats were trapped by the Indians until 1813, on the Mahoning. Bears were very plenty and destructive on hogs as late as 1815. They would seize a hog that would weigh one hundred pounds, in their fore paws, and walk erect with it to the forest. If the hog was too large for them to manage in this manner, they would jump on it, guiding it with their fore feet, and

---

[7] Originally published January 25, February 1, and February 8, 1873

stimulating it by gnawing its neck, thus ride it to the woods and destroy it. A large specimen of the bruin species, engaged in this equestrian exercise was shot by Shadrach Felts (a pioneer still living about one mile west of Lexington on the road to Limaville). Its weight was two hundred pounds. The Bucephalus of its choice was a large hog belonging to Mr. Felts. Bears attack swine by gnawing the tops of their heads and shoulders.

A hog belonging to Nathan Gaskill had strayed away in search of mast, it returned with its eyes out and its skull bone exposed. This hog, though scalped and blinded by bruin lived and was fattened by Gaskill.

The last bear seen in the township was in 1830. A large tract of land that is low and level, consisting of ten or fifteen feet of turfy vegetable deposit, resting on a body of water about three feet deep, upon which East Alliance is now built, was known to the earliest settlement of the township as the "Bear Swamp." This wet, or swamp, land was covered with a dense growth of alder bushes, ten or fifteen feet high, which formed an excellent rendezvous for bears, from it being their covert, it received the name of "Bear Swamp." But there are no alder bushes or swamp or bears there now, and the title is fast losing it significance.

Isaac Teeters — who don't know Isaac? He has been for years an essential feature of the Pittsburgh, Fort Wayne & Chicago Railway at this point. Isaac and Peter Chance, each lost an arm by the premature discharge of an old cast cannon, with which they were trying to give character to a national birthday in Williamsport, over twenty years ago. Isaac well remembers his father, Jonathan, going to this swamp to hunt deer, always returning to his home ladened with bear, deer, or otter.

Deer, in 1806-1807, in Lexington Township, were as abundant as sheep are now, and continued abundant until the great snow storm of 1817, which thawed a little, then froze, this forming a coat which incapacitated them from traveling, hundreds of them starved to death. This protracted snow starved many other varieties of game.

The great snow of 1817 is yet ominously referred to by old people now, but young and vigorous at that date, and battling bravely with the vicissitudes and obstacles of frontier life. The snow averaged a depth of four feet and continued on the ground near four months. Deer could illy[8] travel on the frozen crust of the snow, and if they broke through, they could not extricate themselves, and consequently perished by the score.

Wolves were numerous and the wary and common enemy of the sheep the settlers were trying to introduce, which could only be preserved by penning them up through the night and guarding them through the day.

Turkeys, between the years of 1806 and 1820, were seen in great flocks, often numbering hundreds. A hunter by the name of John Meese, killed out of a single flock, one hundred and eighty, and carried them, realizing in a glutted market a few cents apiece. Porcupines were very thick. They are strictly vegetarian in their habits, living on bark, roots, buds, and wild fruits. There are none now in this section. A price is paid to see them in traveling menageries.

Rabbits and quails were very scarce in early times; these and some other animals are a link between domestic and absolutely wild or untamable animals; they flourish better

---

[8] "Illy" means "not wisely or well; badly"

under the shadow of a sparse population. There are more of them today in the township then there were fifty years ago.

From 1805 to 1820, deer skins were worth seventy-five cents; raccoon skins, twenty-five cents; otter skins, four dollars; and bear skins, one dollar and twenty-five cents.

Rattlesnakes, in early times, in Lexington Township, were quite common, and very numerous. In 1812, one struck an ox above the eye which speedily caused its death. The ox was owned by John Grant, father-in-law to Jonathan Ridgeway Haines. Grant's first cabin was about twenty feet north of Levi L. Lamborn's stable. The debris of the cabin was partially exhumed by the plow last fall. The last rattlesnake seen in the township was caught by the writer in 1850, on the grounds now owned and occupied by the Mount Union College. It was captured by inducing it to enter a barrel laid on its side, and when in, the barrel was straightened up. It was two feet long and had eight rattles. It was kept and experimented with for four months. It took no nourishment during this long time but a small green colored snake, nine inches long. When first captured this snake was very poisonous; it struck a quail on the thigh which caused its death in five minutes. From confinement and improper nourishment, it gradually lost its poisonous qualities.

It is a traditionary practice with hunters traveling grounds infested with this reptile to stuff their boots or shoes with white ash leaves, believing them to be an effectual remedy against the attack of the rattlesnake. So far as this snake was concerned it was found to be but a traditionary practice, for it would dart its head into a bunch of white ash leaves as quickly as it would into a tuft, bush, or elder leaves.

Bees were abundant in the township in early times; wild honey was an article of export second only to maple sugar.

The value of honey from 1806 to 1815, averaged about twelve cents per pound or one dollar per gallon. The pioneers were very expert in ferreting out bee trees. They noticed the direction a bee would take when heavily ladened with the sweets of a wild flower, and that direction would be in a straight line to the hollow tree in which the swarm rendezvoused. The tree, was also found by the drones of the hive which had been killed by the workers and thrown out and lay dead about the roots of the tree. And in the early warm days of the spring the bees would be drawn out of their winter quarters and make a peculiar buzzing noise; these and many other devices were oft resorted to be the sharpened sense of the bee hunter to find this hidden treasure. It is singular how quick the civilized Caucasian becomes an expert in all the shrewd tactics of the savage, to circumvent and capture all kinds of game; these capabilities have been supposed to belong exclusively to the Indian race, but frontier life on the continent has developed many white hunters far superior to any red men of whom we have any account.

Squirrels were not so plentiful at the period of the first settlement of the township, as they were twenty years after. Black squirrels at first were the only ones seen. About 1820, the grey variety made its appearance, and the few that remain at this date are of this kind. In 1840, the red squirrel made its advent into this section and is now altogether the most numerous species.

In 1827, there was a hegira of squirrels; they were so numerous that they destroyed the farmer's crops. There was a squirrel hunt organized this year, a sum or purse of money was raised — the hunters were to receive of this money in proportion to the number of squirrels they shot. They were all to hunt on the same day, and meet in Mt. Union in the evening, count the scalps and receive their *pro rata* of the fund. Job Johnson was purse holder, and Nathan Gaskill, judge. Ellis

N. Johnson, Sr., shot fifty-five, Charles May, 170, etc., and in all they killed in one day seventeen hundred squirrels. Thomas Grant took the premium for killing the greatest number. He now resides in Williams County, Ohio.

In the year 1821, wolves were very numerous and so bold they would attack stock of any kind. A little west of Freedom, on the farm now occupied by Mr. Elisha Teeters, a pack of these animals attacked and killed a cow six years old that belonged to John Grant. About this period the last otters were killed in the Mahoning and its tributaries.

Clayton Grant, now living in Bourbon, Kosciusco County, Indiana, shot the last deer, and caught the last otter seen in Lexington Township.

EARLY SETTLER LIVES AND EXPERIENCES[9]

In the year 1818, a Mr. Hubbard lived one mile east of the Town of Lexington. He, as well as Mrs. Hubbard, were excellent rifle shots, and often amused themselves by shooting at a mark. But death came to the family and left Mrs. Hubbard a widow, with four children depending upon her for the necessities of life.

To illustrate the trials, fortitude, and heroism of a pioneer mother, the following incident is given.

About dusk one evening, a sow that had a brood of pigs by the side of a large log in the woods a little south of Mrs. Hubbard's cabin, was heard demonstrating in a way peculiar to hogs when menaced with danger. Mrs. Hubbard, with the quick sense of a hunter, at once suspected the cause of the

---

[9] Originally published February 8, 1873

threatened peril to the pigs, took her trusty rifle from its resting place and with a courage that would blanch half the men in the township today, went to the scene of trouble; when within a hundred paces, she barely discovered the dim outlines of a great she-wolf battling with the sow. With insufficient light to see the sights upon the gun, she fired. The wolf not knowing from which direction the shot came, or intending to attack her, sprang toward her and fell dead at her feet.

Mrs. Hubbard drew the knife from her hunting girdle, and skinned the wolf, threw the skin over her shoulder and started in the supposed direction of her cabin. In this she was mistaken and bewildered. It was now blank darkness, and she wandered in the woods all that night, and all next day, in the vain search of her humble home and little ones. Again night donned its sable mantle. And to mock its blackness, lit it up with stars, beneath which, and the somber, spectral gloom of arching primitive forests, moved the weary steps, and beat the anxious heart of that brave mother.

After thirty hours of travel and counter travel and circlings in the woods of almost tropical denseness she caught a ray of light which on nearing proved to be a glimmering escaping from between the rude logs of her rustic forest home, though to her more than a palace, for it contained her children, a mother's priceless jewels.

Mrs. Hubbard's second husband was a Hazen by whom she had three children, Daniel, Simeon, and Valentine, uncles to the present generation of Hazens in Lexington Township. This circumstance was related to Ellis N. Johnson by Mrs. Hubbard herself and he thinks he is not mistaken as to her being grandmother to our living citizens of that name. To say the least they are worthy enough to be her offspring, and she was brave enough to be their grandmother.

Up to 1812, salt was very high and scarce; it had to be packed on horseback from Cleveland or Conneaut. The first barrel ever teamed into the township was in 1814 and cost twelve dollars. A few years after this, manufactories of salt were established on Yellow Creek, from which source the early settlers obtained their supplies, at a cost of six dollars a barrel.

The first improvement east of Alliance was on the then called "Mercer Clearing," afterward known as the "Oyster Farm," it is now owned and occupied by James Hoiles. The farm lies at the junction of the County Line Road and the Mt. Union Road.

The only house or cabin in 1818 between Salem and this point was one half a mile this side of Damascus, built and used by a Mr. Morris, who was grandfather to the Hon. James Bruff, who now owns the spot of these primitive improvements.

TOWN OF LEXINGTON[10]

The Town of Lexington was surveyed in lots in 1807, and duly christened after that spot on the continent which witnessed the first contest of British and Colonial arms, and inaugurated the Revolution of 1776.

The name was historical and the anticipations of its founders, doubtless great. By legislative decree the Mahoning was made a public highway of commerce. Provisions were made in the survey for all necessary docks and wharves. Imagination possibly saw the first occupied with masts whose spars floated the flags of other nations, and the latter piled with the exports of the north and the products of the gulf.

---

[10] Originally published February 22, 1873

It can easily be imagined how metropolitan this town, laying claim to such grand expectations, was held by the primitive settlers. Williamsport was not laid out for twenty years thereafter, and then was suburban to Lexington. Freedom followed in twenty-one years, Mt. Union in twenty-three years.

At or soon after the founding of the City of Lexington, President Grant's father lived in the adjoining Township of Deerfield, and was engaged in the tanning business. Captain Oliver, the present Mayor of Alliance, William Vincent, James Garrison, and other citizens attended the National Convention at Chicago in 1868, which nominated for the Chief Executive of the United States, Ulysses S. Grant. The Captain and his comrades went to the headquarters of the Ohio Delegation and found the Deerfield tanner there. They were introduced to the old gentleman, who enquired where they were from. They informed him, from Alliance. He said he had no remembrance of that place or of any of the surrounding towns, which they named. The Captain then told him they lived about midway between Canton and Salem. He then remarked they must be from the Town of Lexington.

NEW GUINEA AND AFRICAN AMERICANS[11]

A colony of colored people located in Lexington Township, one mile east of Williamsport, this being the name of the few buildings on the north side of the Mahoning River, [was known as New Guinea]. This people had a church at the above mentioned point, and they called themselves "Christ's Disciples." All that remains of that church now is a narrow strip of land thrown out to the commons, on the north side of

---

[11] Originally published March 1, 1873

the highway running east, overgrown by brambles. This was their burying ground.

This settlement of colored people comprised about two hundred souls, and was made up chiefly of fugitives and freedmen from Virginia. They were orderly, industrious, and esteemed good citizens.

Messrs. I. Price, Roland Bracy and E. Hamlin officiated in the church in the administration of the Word.

An anecdote is related to one of their preachers, as occurring in the heated summary of his discourse, establishing that doctrine that they were God's peculiar people. He touchingly referred to the lamb-like tufts of wool upon their heads as conclusive upon the point that they were his special lambs.

This church and settlement is now, and has been for years, entirely broken up. From this point two fugitives were recaptured and consigned to a life of hopeless toil. Logan County, in this state, and Lower Canada, were the two chief points to which they emigrated.

In 1850, there were only thirty-nine colored residents in Lexington Township. In 1860, there were one hundred and fifty-seven, thirty-eight in the Limaville Precinct and one hundred and nineteen in the Alliance Precinct. In 1870, there were two hundred and one colored citizens in the township; sixty-six in the Limaville Precinct, and one hundred and thirty-four in the Alliance Precinct.

This people possess in a large degree the religious element. They have now a church in Alliance, organized in 1870, by "Uncle Josie Armstrong," a colored man of large brain, and possessing great power as a preacher and great unction in prayer. This organization is called the African Methodist

Church; it has no regular pastor at present and is languishing; embracing only from fifteen to twenty members.

EARLY CABIN CONSTRUCTION[12]

Prior to 1812, there was no necessity for sawed lumber in the township. The floors of the cabins were made of "puncheons," their roofs were covered with "clapboards," rived from the straight grained oak timbers, their sides of round logs, their doors of heavy clapboards and swung on wooden hinges.; their windows consisted of a couple of feet cut from one of the side logs and the hole covered with greased paper. The chimney and fireplace was a magnificent affair. The latter often occupying the entire end of the cabin and the base of it was built of hard black stones or "bog oar," and the balance of the chimney above the contact of the first was built on the outside of the cabin, of cross sticks and tempered clay. These cabins made of one room were one story high and a "loft." The furniture consisted of a rude table and stools of primitive style. In some instances there were two doors in the same cabin directly opposite, and logs ten feet long and eighteen inches in diameter were drawn with a horse into the cabin and then rolled into the capacious fireplace. A few green logs of this size when fairly ablaze would bid defiance to the coldest weather.

This form of cabin architecture was followed, not precisely by the Corinthian style, but by an improved hewed log house. The logs were flatted on both sides, the joists were hewed, the flooring sawed, and the buildings were mostly two stories high; the roofs were made of riveted and often shaved oaken shingles, fastened to the sheeting with nails which would now

---

[12] Originally published March 1, 1873

be obtained at twenty-five cents per pound. The windows were few but consisted of a four-light sash window made to hold 8 x 10 glass; the crevices between the logs were filled by juggles and then neatly plastered on the in and outside with a well tempered yellow clay, of which article there has never been any scarcity in the township. The outside ponderous chimney of the round-log cabin was moved to the inside of the hewed log house. This kind of house was warm and neat and also "aristocratic," until John Grant in 18 – , built a commodious two-story brick house, west and across the ravine from where Amos Coates now lives.

VILLAGE OF MT. UNION[13]

*"When you and I were young, Bob,
Just twenty years ago."*

The Lexington side of Mt. Union was surveyed into lots in 1826, by Job Johnson, Esq., and Richard Webb, who were also owners of the land on the north side of the State Road. In the same year, Job Johnson opened the first store in the place, which had been successively kept by Johnson, Pettit & Wilson, J. M. Pettit, and Pettit & Park. On the northeast corner, a store was successfully run a number of years by V. Millhouse & Co.

A tavern was opened by Job Johnson in the place. J. B. Nixon followed on the southwest corner with a public house. John Hair opened one on the southeast corner.

"Taverns," before the era of railroads, were the main features of a village. Mt. Union supported two, Williamsport one, Freedom two, Lexington three, and Limaville two. The railway cuts off all patronage to taverns in the villages, but a

---

[13] Originally published March 22, 1873

stray peddler, or a perambulating stock man, or a patent right dealer.

The building formerly occupied by Mr. J. B. Nixon, as a hotel, was consumed by fire a few years back. Mr. Edward Conn is occupant in the Hair corner, and is well patronized and meritoriously, as reputation ascribes to his tables all the qualities a hungry and even fastidious taste desires. Mr. Judd, has erected a fine building, during the past year, on Main Street, directly south of the college building, designing it for student boarders, and the accommodations of the public. The Mount presents quite a lifelike appearance during the college term, but the vacation makes it sufficiently rural and quiet, for the most fastidious recluse. Commencement days, are gala days in the village; they are its Fourth of Julys; crowds of visitors throng to the College; students away for a year or two, or more, return to their Alma-Mater, and revivify old acquaintances, carrying with them the exuberant spirits of youth, and the high hopes common to the morn of existence, common to all before the battle of life is lost or won. Twenty-five years ago, Mt. Union was inhabited by a lively set of young men. They are now scattered through different states, and the vicissitudes of life and the weight of years, have sobered many of them into influential citizens.

They had the practice of giving each other nick-names and persistently calling their comrades by the same. These per names were given in mirth, and received in good feeling, but so persistently were those names applied, and so tenaciously were they adhered to that they are known by them still, although over a quarter a century has passed since they were thus christened. It is believed that no offence will be given in alluding to some of the names and the parties to whom they were applied. Of those of this coterie who have sought their fortunes in distant states, some have attained a little eminence. Joseph Hoiles has filled a position as members of the

Nebraska Legislature. B. W. Johnson was a member of the Iowa Legislature. John H. Long, was elected to the Indiana Legislature. Joseph Dilworth, and Ellis N. Johnson, have both been members of the Ohio Legislature.

Dr. Dilworth is in the successful practice of medicine in the Mount. Dr. R. P. Johnson had a fine practice in the City of Alliance. Dr. John H. Long of Indiana gives his attention to surgery, the two latter, held commissions as surgeons in the Army and all three of them received their private medical instructions from Levi L. Lamborn.

"Fulton," is a very successful school teacher.

"Beeswax," is an efficient professor in a college.

"Bullion," practices physics.

"Joe Athens," is an extensive stock dealer.

"Heckernel," is a legislator.

"Stone Burner," was a fine prognosticator of the weather, and is operating Post Master.

"Wooley Hooker," farmed in Washington Township, and always took his politics straight through all the vicissitudes of Whiggery down.

"Ben Durgans," tickles the fertile soil of Wood County, with his plow, and it laughs for him in sheaves of golden grain. (Don't let anyone be misled by thinking that sentence is original.)

"Toot," is President of a flourishing college.

"Doctor," lives quietly in Orrville.

"Burge," was the first Mayor of Alliance.

"Trussler," farms in Iowa.

Chapter tenth[14], although unmeaning to more recent settlers in Lexington Township, was keenly relished by those whose memories led them back to the incidents and locality to which it referred. It unlocked the portals of hallowed reminiscences and continued the passwords to the charmed circle of youth as it was "twenty years ago."

It has been requested that a few more aliases of that era be quoted into the immortality of history.

"Keefer," carried on the wagon making business, and is Justice of the Peace of Washington Township.

"Major," lives on Mt. Union Street, as is evidenced by the scores of dilapidated wagons and buggies around his premises awaiting repairs.

"Ludwick," is a chicken fancier, and runs a live grocery & provision business on Broadway, Alliance.

"Glaspy," farms on Beech Creek, Lexington Township.

"Boger" and "Bebb," both live in the West.

This list of pet names might be extended but enough are given to illustrate the practice of the locality, and to awaken a pleasant reminiscence of the past, in the mind of anyone who remembers the parties to whom those names were applied.

---

[14] Originally published March 29, 1873, as an Addenda to the week's article

MORE ABOUT THE VILLAGE OF MT. UNION[15]

The first grapevine in Lexington Township was planted by Job Johnson in Mt. Union, on the east side of the building he erected, and for a long period thereafter known as Pettit's store. The vine is in good condition, and annually bears its full quantity of fruit, of the Isabella variety.

The first physician in Mt. Union was Dr. Joseph Shreve. He died of a cancerous development on the neck. He was succeeded by his brother-in-law, Dr. Caleb Jones, who practiced in the village for a number of years, when he removed to Massillon, and there deceased. Levi L. Lamborn followed Dr. Jones, and Dr. Joseph Dilworth, now fairly and meritoriously occupies the ground. A Dr. Teeters, was in the village two or three years; also Dr. Woodruff, and a few other transient and Esculapean devotees, have "swallow-like, come and gone."

The first Temperance meeting in Lexington Township was held in the grove adjoining the Village of Mt. Union, in 1826, by Dr. Thomas C. Shreve, of Deerfield, Dr. Joseph Shreve, of Mt. Union, and Ellis N. Johnson, Sr., one of the proprietors of the village on the Washington Township side, who officiated as speakers. Prior to this date, the propriety of the use of spirituous liquors was never questioned by the settlers of the township. The use of whiskey at raisings, log rollings, and butchering were considered essential.

About the year 1852-1853, a traveling show came to the Village of Mt. Union. The proprietor was a man of considerable capability and learning. He illustrated by adapted appliances the power and the laws governing

---

[15] Originally published March 22, 1873

electricity. He had two veritable Egyptian mummies, and various other novel and interesting articles on exhibition. He exhibited one night very acceptably to the citizens, and notified the people of his design to repeat the performance with some change of programme on the following evening. He was, on the second evening, greeted with a full house. About the time he was to commence his illustrations, he stepped out of the door as if for a moment's absence, and was never seen or heard of afterwards. The following day the surrounding country was searched for his discovery without avail. The mummies, etc., were left to be cared for by the citizens for some months, when the whereabouts of his wife was discovered, and the exhumed denizens of Cheops were shipped to her.

DR. JOHN SHREVE[16]

"He was a man, take him for all in all;
We ne'er shall look upon his like again."

William Shakespeare, Hamlet

"Whose distant footsteps echo
Through the corridors of time;"

Edgar Allen Poe, The Poetic Principle

John Shreve died at Mt. Union, September 8th, 1854, aged ninety two years and five months. Dr. Joseph Shreve was a son of his and the first physician in Mount Union. Dr. Shreve was a man of generous impulses and broad sympathies. He died of cancerous disease of the neck. With a full knowledge of his approaching death, he sent for James English, a man with whom he had some difficulties and a full reconciliation

---

[16] Originally published April 26, 1873

was affected, and the doctor asked him to seal the settlement of their difficulties by throwing upon his coffin the first shovel full of earth. Mr. English acceded to this eccentric request and discharged his promise.

John Shreve had four other sons, two of whom were physicians, Solomon and Thomas. The first practiced his profession for many years in Damascus. His wife was a sister to Isaac Coates, a citizen of this township, by whom he had several children. This branch of the Shreve family are all deceased, except Mr. Henry Shreve, the present excellent postmaster in the city of Alliance. Thomas Shreve practiced medicine in Deerfield a number of years, after which he removed to the city of Massillon. After residing there a few years he removed to the west. His other two sons Israel and Benjamin are still living in, or near Salem, Columbiana County, Ohio. Dr. Caleb Jones married Eliza Shreve, a daughter of John Shreve and practiced many years in Mt. Union, from which place he removed to Massillon and there deceased. Dr. Jones' widow with an unmarried sister, Mary, now resides in Salem.

John Shreve was a man of extraordinary vigor of mind and was universally respected by all with whom he came in contact. He was born in Burlington County, New Jersey, April 8th, 1762; thirteen years before the Declaration of Independence. His father Israel Shreve was Lieut. Colonel of the second Regiment from New Jersey in that war. His father's regiment was ordered to Quebec, and young John accompanied it. In December 1776, John Shreve, then 14 years old, was commissioned ensign of the 2nd Regiment New Jersey volunteers, and his father promoted to a colonelcy. On the following July, John was promoted to a lieutenancy and was in many engagements of the war. A narrative of the revolution was published by John Shreve in 1854[17], from which the following quotation is made, relative to the treason and execution of Andre.

"The enemy sent a twenty-two gun ship up the river Hudson, having on board their Adjutant General, John Andre, the spy. She came to anchor at the head of Tappan Bay, about seven miles below West Point. Andre landed, had an interview with Major General Benedict Arnold, who conducted him to West Point Forts, and gave him a plan of the forts and public works. When that ship took her station so near the highlands and the Fort, the New Jersey Brigade was ordered up to the village of Orangetown. Here we met General Green with several brigades of New England troops.

I was ordered, with a sergeant, corporal, and twenty-four privates, to take a stand on the west side of the bay, nearly opposite where the ship lay, to watch her motions and prevent her having intercourse with the shore. I was then about three miles above Orangetown, and was to remain there one week unless sooner recalled. After being there a few days I saw a barge, rowed by four men, with two sitting in the stern sheets, go to the ship. She immediately weighed anchor, made sail, and passed down the river, with a full band of music playing. Before she got out of sight, another boat came out of the narrows, from West Point, rowed by four men, and two in the stern. She passed by us and landed at the mouth of a small stream called "the Slote." She was the guard boat from West Point, commanded by Lieut. Edes, with information to General Green that Major John Andre had been taken on a horse, within a short distance of the British lines, with a plan

---

[17] *The Genealogy and History of the Shreve Family* from 1641, by Luther Prentice Allen, available on Google Books, indicates the account was written in November 1853.

of the fort and works, in the hand-writing of the traitor, General Benedict Arnold. Major Andre called himself John Anderson. He had a pass from Arnold under that name. He was taken by three militia-men and conveyed to an American officer, at an outpost, who suffered him to write a letter to Arnold, under the name of John Anderson, informing him that he was taken prisoner. General Arnold made his escape to the British ship. I was then recalled and joined the regiment.

General Washington returned at that time from Rhode Island, where he had an interview with the French Admiral De Grasse. General Washington then sent Major Andre to Orangetown, to General Green, and called in the Governor of New York and the militia to keep possession of West Point. Not knowing the extent of the conspiracy among the troops that General Arnold had had under his command, Washington sent them to General Green, as soon as he had made preparations to repair the breaches that Arnold had made in several of the fortifications while Andre was there. Arnold's excuse for this was, that he wanted to make alterations for their better security.

The British intended to attack West Point as soon as Major Andre returned from there with the plans of the fortifications.

After General Washington arrived at Orangetown, where the greater part of our army were collected, he ordered a court martial of the general officers, to try Major Andre. They pronounced him a spy, and by the articles of war he ought to suffer death by hanging. General Washington approved the sentence, and appointed a day for it to be carried into effect.

The prisoner was guarded by a captain, two subalterns, and sixty privates.

"I was not on duty the day of the execution and when the guard moved from the place of confinement with the prisoner, I joined them. Shortly we came in full view of the gallows and a great number of citizens and soldiers collected to witness the execution. Andre did not appear to be the least confused and was in familiar conversation with the captain and one of the guards. On looking forward, Andre saw the gallows and remarked, "I am fully reconciled to my fate, but am disappointed in the mode." He said he had petitioned Washington to die like a soldier, and that he could not bear the idea of dying on a gibbet. He then again commenced the conversation which the sight of the gallows had broken off.

When we arrived at the spot, the detachment under the command of my father, that had formed around the gallows to keep off the crowd, opened to the right and left to let us through. There was a wagon under the gallows with a coffin in it. Andre stepped up into the wagon. General Parsons was officer of the day. He rode up and read the sentence of the court martial, and looking at his watch, said: "Major Andre, you have fifteen minutes to live—if you wish to say anything you have now an opportunity." Andre replied: "I have nothing to say, but this is for you to bear witness, that I meet my fate like a brave man." He then took a white handkerchief out of his pocket, and pulled off his scarlet coat, giving it to his servant and telling him to go and put it in his trunk. The servant immediately left for that purpose, the tears running down his cheeks.

The wagon moved on to let Andre swing clear. When dead, he was taken down, put into the coffin and driven under an escort to the landing place at the river, where a boat belonging to the enemy was in waiting, and by permission, was taken to the British camp at New York, arriving there about midnight. He was not buried under or near the gallows, as some historians have asserted.

Early Residents

JOHN AND JESSE GRANT AND DEERFIELD[18]

"Some then are born great, others, achieve greatness, some, have greatness thrust upon them"

William Shakespeare, Twelfth Night

Among the early settlers of Lexington Township, the name of John Grant must not be omitted. He came into the Township in 1809, lived one year in the Town of Lexington, and in 1810, he built a cabin a few rods northwest of the present residence of Levi L. Lamborn, on the quarter of land he entered, the northeast corner of which is at the junction of the Mt. Union Road with the Pittsburgh, Fort Wayne & Chicago Railway. He afterward built the first brick house in Lexington Township a few rods south of the present residence of his son-in-law Mr. Jonathan Ridgeway Haines, on the same quarter. Mr. David Rockhill "off-bore" the brick for that house. It was torn down and the south wing of Mr. Haines' residence is constructed out of the same brick, the first ever made in the township.

---

[18] Originally published March 29, 1873

John Grant died at the residence of his son-in-law, Mr. Haines, fifteen-years ago. He was a man of singular will power and tenacity of purpose. He has two daughters still living in the township, Mrs. Jonathan Ridgeway Haines and Mrs. Simon Huffer. Stacy Grant, a son of his, died a few years ago back, two miles west of Alliance. Clayton Grant, a son of his, lives in Bourbon, Indiana, and also Thomas Grant, a son lives near Unity, Williams County, Ohio.

Mr. John Grant came to Lexington from New Jersey. A few years after his advent into this township, Jesse Grant, his first cousin[19] came from New Jersey and settled in Deerfield Township, Portage County, the first township northeast of Lexington. Jesse Grant is living at present in Covington, Kentucky, and is father of Ulysses S. Grant, the acting President of the United States. Jesse Grant engaged in the tanning business in Deerfield in a small way, having about six vats from 1812 to 1820. He removed at the latter date from Deerfield farther west, but has frequently revisited the location of his first embarkation in business. His last visit to see his friends and early acquaintances in this locality was 1871.

By the kindness of Mr. John Day, at present engaged with Mr. Reed in this city, the son of Capt. Alva Day (deceased), but a resident of Deerfield at the time, to whom the letters were directed, I am enabled to present two autograph letters of the venerable Jesse Grant, dated Maysville, Kentucky. These letters will explain themselves. The superscription tells that the rate of postage from Maysville, Kentucky, to Deerfield,

---

[19] Genealogical research has since discovered that Jesse and John Grant were not cousins. Jesse Grant and his family came from Connecticut, not New Jersey. – R.H.

Ohio, was twenty-four cents. The chirography is in clever style, for fifty-eight years ago.

It might be proper to state that the Ely referred to, is a relative of our excellent friend Linus Ely, and the Farnam mentioned in the letter is the man who first carried mail through Lexington Township. Mr. Alva Day was a captain in the War of 1812. Jesse Grant was probably not over 21 years of age when those letters were written.

Maysville, March 15th, 1815

Capt. A. Day.

Dear Sir:

I arrived here on Saturday, after a passage of three days and a half in a skiff, and since I arrived I have ridden into the country considerable, and have made inquiry about sheep and wool, and I believe that it would not answer well to convey wool or drive sheep to Deerfield. I find that sheep have sold here, in the winter, for from 10 to 18 shillings per head, and in the wool factories, they have advertised three shillings per pound for wool, but it is thought that peace will affect a material change in the price of wool and sheep. There has been a considerable quantity of dry goods and merchandise of all kinds landed here since my arrival that were purchased since the peace, and they are now sold. They are cheaper than they were before the war, and this of course must reduce the price of wool and sheep, very much so that by next season, it would answer a good purpose to come here and purchase a drove of sheep to drive to your county.

I would now inform you that I have made my calculations to return to Deerfield in the fall, and settle myself, and I now wish you to see to getting me some bark, do not fail of having 6, 8, or 10 cords of bark got for me. Mr. Ely and Mr. Forman will probably get some, as they are going to clear land this spring. I wish you to use your influence in my behalf and get and save me all of the hides and calf skins that you can, and save and preserve them in the way that I directed you when I was there. I wish you to inform the citizens of the place generally that I shall be back, that they may reserve their hides for me. I shall be back in September, and will bring $200 worth of leather in the rough, and about $150 in cash, and I shall endeavor to drive on the business with all possible rapidity. My neglect of writing to my brother when I was in Deerfield, caused him to fear that I was not coming back again, and he entered into partnership with Mr. Grimes, the forenoon before my return, but they had not entered into articles, and he offered me the refusal of the chance. I have been there four days studying on it, and have finally concluded to return to Deerfield. I will write you an order in this letter on Esq. Menary, for that money of mine that is in his hands, and I want you to put it into use by purchasing hides, and the first time you see Esq. Lewis, I wish you to enquire if Mr. Hadley has entered bail, if not, I want you to take out an execution immediately, and have that money collected as soon as possible. You will hear from me again in a few mails, by a letter to Merrick Ely.

I wish you would speak to the managers of the Atwater sawmill for about 6 poplar planks, of the length and size of those now in the old shop, and oak plank enough to make a table 10 feet in length and three feet, 6 or 8 inches in width and 4 inches thick; two planks of 21 or 22 inches in width if they can be got, would answer best for the table, but if they are not to be had of that width, there must be three, but two would be the best. These I wish to have got as soon as possible, and stuck up to dry, that they may not be sun-cracked. If you will take the trouble of this business on yourself, I will endeavor to make you satisfied for it when I return, beside being very much obliged to you.

Please give my best respects to your family and all enquirers if any there be.

Capt. Alva Day. Yours with respect,

JESSE GRANT

———

Maysville, March 18th, 1815

Mr. John Menary:

Sir, please to pay to the bearer, Alva Day, when it is collected, all of the money that is coming to me of Mr. Thaddeus Granger, and this shall be your receipt for the same.

JESSE GRANT

———

I wish you to write me an answer soon and let me know what luck in business.

J. G. [JESSE GRANT]

———

Maysville, May 21st, 1815

Capt. A. Day.

 Sir:

Yours of the 7th of April came safely to hand in good time, which brought the pleasing intelligence of health, etc. I neglected answering yours for some time. When I received a letter from Merrick Ely, I should then have answered yours, but father was from home at my sister's a distance of 8 or 9 miles, and as I wanted him to be at home to write an order to Esq. Menary, I deferred writing until the present time, and he has not yet come back, but as I consider that it may be of some importance that you should hear from me. I have concluded to write without him. I wish you to inform Mr. Menary that I cannot conscientiously wait any longer on Mr. Granger, and that I wish him to collect the money as soon as possible. I should not care to wait until fall for the money if I could send any up to you for the purpose of buying skins, etc., but as that cannot be done with safety, "what can't be cured, must be endured." I must get you to apologize to my

———

friend, Mr. Granger, for my necessity of having the money now, but placing confidence in his goodness I have hopes of being excused. You inform him (whilst mentioning the necessity of an order from my father) that the Esq. would pay you the money by your securing him from harm, which I wish you would do, as you would confer a singular favor on me, and as you will have the money in your hands you will be secure from harm yourself.

You wrote that you thought that you could get me some skins, which I wish you would do, be careful to have them dry on the hair before you hang them up, then dust them on the flesh side and hang them in the shade and they will keep until fall, without any damage. I want you to secure all the hides and skins that you can on the shares, and purchase such as you can't get on the shares while the money lasts, and if you will furnish some when mine fails, I will replace it on my return, with interest.

I shall be in Deerfield in September. I do not expect you will have an opportunity to secure many hides previous to that time, but I am in hopes that you will secure as many as you can. You informed me that you had bespoke the plank, but I was very sorry to observe your letter entirely silent on the subject of bark. However, that sorrow was somewhat removed by Mr. Ely's letter in which he stated that he intended to peel me some himself. What is peeled for me I wish to have drawn and put in the bark mill, for the season is so wet that I am afraid it will all be spoiled, and that would prove a serious damage to me.

The money that Mr. Hadley owes me, will become payable in July, and I wish you to have it collected immediately.

I wish you to write to me as soon as you get this and let me know what quantity of bark you have got me, and what the chance will be for hides and skins.

You wrote that you had received a letter from my father, and that the contents of it, justified you in flattering yourself that you would see him in Deerfield, this summer. I believe that it is his intention to go up, but do not think it would be advisable, as he is so old and infirm, that I fear he could not stand the fatigue of the journey. Since I returned, he appears to be discontented here, and wants to go with me, and I believe if he was there, he would want to get back as much as ever. It is, however, a little uncertain as to his going, but brother Noah will come with me.

I have no news to write, and have probably already written more than you will want to read, so I must conclude by requesting you to give my best respects to your family, and all of my acquaintances, and accept the same yourself.

I remain yours with sentiment of esteem.

Alva Day Esq.

JESSE GRANT

P. S. Please inform Merrick Ely, that I have received his letter, for which I return him my sincere thanks and best respects.

J. GRANT

RECOLLECTIONS OF ELLIS N. JOHNSON[20]

"To know nothing of the past is always to remain a child" – *Cicero*

"Fifty years beside this same fireplace"

There is nothing so well calculated to impress one's mind with the untiring perseverance and indomitable energy of the "Yankee Nation," as to trace in the detail the opening history of a single township. In viewing the giant progress of the nation, in the aggregate, the mind is bewildered with the innumerable agents at play, in unfolding its illimitable resources; and consequently cannot grasp and estimate correctly the mighty achievements of that unyielding, iron will, which is the birthright of all Americans.

The genius of our pioneer ancestry and their posterity, is boldly shadowed forth, when we reflect that fifty years have scarce elapsed since the wide solitude of an unbroken forest was interrupted by the howl of the wolf, the scream of the panther, and the yell of the savage Indian! Scarce half a century has passed since these graceful, undulating, productive fields, now bearing the choicest agricultural productions in rich profusion, were dark, impenetrable forests, whose boughs were tangled and confused in a rayless, overarching dome. Fifty years ago, the grassy knolls on the

---

[20] Originally published March 8 & 15, 1873

sequestered Mahoning, that are now the embowered and romantic seats of eager fishermen, were the sunning spots of the luxuriant otter and the dome of the provident beaver's home.

Ellis N. Johnson, Sr., whose age now approximates 90 years, still lives in the west end of the Village of Mt. Union, just across the south line of Lexington Township, in Washington Township.

Ellis N. Johnson, Sr. on his 100th birthday

We visited him one evening a few weeks back to gather from him his memories of former years. On entering his house he saluted the writer with the remark, "Well here I am as I have been for fifty years, beside this same fireplace."

His health is good, memory fresh and step steady. For a number of years he filled the office of Justice of the Peace. He has also acted as attorney before justice courts in the surrounding townships, and as Notary Public, and in his time has done an immense amount of intermediate business in the way of contracts, settlements, and adjustments of difficulties between the people of his neighborhood. He has also done a large amount of surveying in this and adjoining counties.

Mr. Johnson has been a practical surveyor all his life and a reasonable inference would be that he would have more than ordinary aptness in determining directions and the cardinal points of the compass. But the old gentleman tells circumstance of being lost in the forests in early times, which will illustrate, first, the bewilderment or confusion of the senses common to persons under such circumstances; second, his style of farming; third, the vein of genial mirth which always characterizes him.

After wandering in the woods for hours he approached an improvement with a cabin and log stable; he says everything appeared strange, the fences were very poor, and their directions marked with broad belts of vines. The stable was in a bad state of repair, the stumpy fields were badly tilled. After a time the idea dawned upon his mind that this might be his home, he thought he would enter the stable and see if he could recognize his horses; horses like his were there, but they were poor, the stalls were divided by rails elevated at the front end, and the horses were elevated at the hind end by a season's undisturbed pile of valuable compost, and there was left but little provender in the loft. He bethought him to impose a further test of his ownership, and that was to enter the cabin, and if Dorcas, his wife, was there it would be strongly circumstantial; if she recognized him as her liege lord it would be conclusive to his identity; this attempt dispelled all illusions.

Mr. Johnson came to Ohio from Washington County, Pennsylvania, in 1813, and deadened ten acres on the farm he now occupies, and ten acres on his brother Simon's farm one mile south of Mt. Union, and ten acres on his brother Caleb's farm one mile east of the village. He moved on the farm in the fall of 1823, built a cabin on the site of his present residence and the cabin fireplace was on the spot now occupied by the grate fire in his common sitting room; so his feet have been on the same hearthstone for nearly fifty years of time. Caleb Johnson, his brother, followed him from Washington County in the spring of 1824. Joseph Johnson, his cousin, entered the farm he yet lives on one mile west of Alliance in the spring of 1823, and Job Johnson, his youngest brother, bought the farm of 160 acres now owned by Mr. William A. Nixon, and on which a part of the town of Mt. Union is built, in 1825, for $600.

Caleb Johnson died years ago leaving sons and daughters; Job died in Pennsylvania; Simon, Ellis Johnson's youngest brother, died in Alliance a few years back, leaving as children, B. W. Johnson, who lives in Iowa, and is, or has been, a member of the legislature of that state; Simon Johnson, who was the [fifth][21] Mayor of Alliance and at present a Justice of the Peace of Lexington Township; Dr. R. P. Johnson, is a practicing physician in the City of Alliance and has a fine reputation in the "noble art of healing." Z. B. Johnson keeps a large livery or

---

[21] Lamborn erroneously labeled him as the first mayor of Alliance.

sale stable in Alliance, and has the name of being the best judge of a horse in Stark County. Of their daughters, "Mell" is married and lives in Chattanooga; Rebecca lives in Iowa; "Mark K." lives in Canton, the wife of Josiah Hartzell, the able editor of the *Republican and Repository*, one of the best county papers published in Ohio. Kesiah, the relist of Simon Johnson with an older and unmarried daughter lived with Dr. Johnson in this city.

"Nothing so dear as a tale of the olden time."

The difference being so great between the surroundings of life in Lexington Township fifty years ago and what they are today, many might conclude that those old veterans of pioneer life, had deprivations and hardships without any interims of pleasure. Such a conclusion is very wide of the mark; they had their recreations and festivals. The brain power and moral tension for wealth was not so great then, and more frequently relaxed than it is today. Democracy pervades society in frontier life, wealth and development are the lever-arms upon which aristocracy treads to power. Democracy is equality and humanity, border and dependent life compels it. Aristocracy is enthroned selfishness, wealth and its purchases permit it.

The pioneers, outside of superior social enjoyment common among early settlers, enjoyed a delirious pleasure when, with their sinewy arms, they grappled with the ferocious bear. They felt a wild enjoyment when the fleeting stag fell dead in his lightning course, through the agency of their unerring rifles. This exhilarating and manly sport may be startling to the pampered effeminate sons of luxury. Those iron-armed, resolute settlers might have been unlearned in books, but they were wise and ennobled from an admitted converse and intimacy with nature, when her grandeur was undefaced by man's spoiling art.

Mr. Ellis N. Johnson, Sr., gave the following incident, somewhat indefinitelyness as to the year the circumstances occurred in. In the year 1820, a family by the name of Pound, lived on the northern boundary of Lexington Township. They had two children, a little girl and boy, aged respectively six and eight years. One evening in August, they sent the children for the cows, which were some distance south of the cabin in the forest. The parents soon found the sound of bells on the cattle receding from them in the woods. They went after the cattle and overtook them, but could find nothing of the children.

They made what little search they could that night for the children by traversing the woods, one or two neighbors assisting them, but without success. The next morning they obtained all the assistance they could from the neighborhood, which was sparsely settled, and the woods were searched that day without finding the children. In the evening, however, messengers were sent to the surrounding towns, and even as far as Canton, for assistance to search the woods. They were to meet the following morning at Pound's cabin, which they did in numbers of about one hundred. They then regularly organized by appointing captains and lieutenants, and arranged themselves in an east and west line, in calling distance of each other.

The captains had horns; one sound of which signified to dress line; two sounds were to indicate some signs of the missing children; three blasts were to be the signal of their discovery. The line of men started in a southern direction and marched until they searched a point as far south as Alliance, about five miles from the place of starting, when they discovered imprints of the children's feet in the sand of Beech Creek, on the Shaffer farm. The march however was continued until they reached a line corresponding with the east and west road two miles south of Mt. Union, in Washington Township.

There was a deadening on the land directly west of the farm now owned and occupied by Richard Lee, late Commissioner of Stark County. This clearing had grown up thickly with blackberry bushes, at this season ladened with ripe fruit. The deer had made paths in several directions through these bushes. At the entrance of one of these, in the mire, the hunters discovered the recent impress of the children's feet. The searching party felt assured that the missing children were in this covert of bushes. The line was called in, and surrounded this opening which embraced about ten acres. The searching parties entered by these paths.

The little girl was soon discovered, but was so wild that no entreaties could induce her to come towards the men, but rapidly fled across them. She was soon overtaken and caught, but had apparently lost the power of speech; she could not, or would not give any information on the missing brother. After the search being continued for some time, he was discovered sleeping beside a fallen tree, and he was equally irreconcilable.

The children were stained with berries, and their garments almost torn from their bodies by the brambles of the forest. West of the thicket where the children were found, on the farm now owned by Mr. Shaffer, in a log cabin, then lived Isaac Dinsmore, to whose humble home the hunters with the children repaired. The children refused to take any nourishment; mother Dinsmore said they must eat, and attempted to force feed food in their mouths. After a couple of hours of rest and delay, two of the fleetest horsemen of the expedition, took each of them a child and returned them rapidly to their home, which was eight miles distant through the unbroken forest.

The parents of the children had remained at the home. The children on their arrival were taken into the cabin of their parents, but refused to talk or to recognize them. There were two doors in the cabin, and the first opportunity that offered, the children darted like young Indians through the back door into the woods again. They were caught and brought back but had to be constantly watched for some time to prevent them from escaping. A number of days elapsed before their bewilderment and partial lunacy left them, and they recognized their parents and resumed the power of speech.

STORIES FROM EARLY SETTLERS[22]

David Kendrick, in early times lived in a cabin on what has been known as the Garwood farm, recently owned by Joshua Garwood, purchased of him by Jehu B. Milner, and surveyed into town lots and christened as Milner's third addition to Alliance.

David Kendrick went to Friends meetings at Lexington, often taking with him his son Nelson, a little boy three years old. On his way home a violent storm arose, and about the junction of Main and Mt. Union Streets, a tree blew down killing Nelson and breaking Mr. Kendrick's leg in two places. He was carried to the cabin of Mr. Perry Chance, situated about the present location of Mr. Lower's brick residence just north of the Pittsburgh, Fort Wayne & Chicago Railway.

About 1850, the wheat raised in Lexington Township was diseased, producing an affection of the human system, known as "wheat sickness." The grains of wheat were plump, and to all appearances healthy, but the flour when baked left a pungent taste in the throat, and produced a deathly nausea

---

[22] Originally published May 17, 1873

and vomiting. Wheat, rye, and other cereal grains, prior to 1825, were cleaned by bouncing them in a sheet in a current of wind, the four corners being held by two persons; but at the above date windmills were introduced, and the grain tramped out with the horses or cattle on barn floor, or threshed with a flail up to 1845, when threshing machines were introduced. A few years after this the improvements were attached to the threshers, so that grain was delivered from the machine ready cleaned for the market.

Mrs. Nancy Rockhill, at present living with her son-in-law, John Q. Ramsey, left her cabin on the present site of the residence of Clement Rockhill, her son, to visit Joseph Johnson, still living and residing two miles west of Alliance. In returning to her home in the evening she got lost in the forest, though the neighbors went to her rescue with horns and lanterns, she was not found till the following morning.

It will be a source of pleasure to all the old settlers of the township, to read the following letter from Clayton Grant, of Bourbon, Indiana.

Mr. Grant was well and favorably known by them all prior to his removal to the west.

Mr. Littleberry Stanley, alluded to the letter as one of the parties at the squirrel hunt, was reputed as one of the finest marksmen in the township, and was father to our excellent and energetic citizen T. G. Stanley.

———

Bourbon, Ind., March 22nd, 1873

Mr. Ridgeway Haines:

Dear Sir:

Your letter of the _____ inst. came duly to hand, asking some questions about my recollection of early times in Lexington Township. By tradition, I understand that John Grant, my father, settled on the farm on which you now reside in 1809. I was born there in 1811. In 1812, we moved to a house where Lexington now stands; when the war was over, we moved back to the old place. The first grist mill built in that township was built about the year 1826, near where the Town of Limaville now stands, afterwards known as Sage's mill. It was built by Joseph Elliott. Afterwards, in about 1821, John Pennock built one where Williamsport was then commenced.

John Mace[23] was one of the early settlers of Lexington Township, he settled on what was, and perhaps is, still known as the old Oyster farm, on the Salem Road due east of Mt. Union about two miles, it was said that while he lived there that he killed thirty bears. Many others were killed along the Mahoning and its tributaries. I recollect of my father and his boys killing four of them along that little run that passes through the farm on which Clem Rockhill now lives.

I carried up one of the corners of the first house built in Mt. Union on the Lexington side, about the year 1828 or 1829. About the year 1830, I built a cellar wall for my brother Thomas, afterwards occupied by William Teeters. The place is now occupied by Alliance. From 1833 to 1838, I lived in the east side of what is now Alliance, cleared the land, built the first cabin there, and lived happy in it for those five years.

---

[23] This is likely John Meese, ed.

Father built his brick house on the old farm about the year 1826, and his barn about 1828. The great squirrel hunt of which you inquire came off about the year 1832. Littleberry Stanley took the first prize and I took second. I think he killed about eighty, and I about seventy-five that day. The last deer that I have any knowledge of being killed in those parts, I first saw shot and wounded about 1½ miles southwest of Mt. Union; I had a horse with me, the deer ran northwest about three miles, I rode until I came to Brother Stacy's place, where the widow now lives, hitched my horse to his fence, where he stayed till the next day. I followed the deer till he turned back, then back we went 2½ miles to near the starting point, then a straight shot for Mt. Union, passed through the edge of it, thence through where Alliance now is situated, on to Fish Creek, thence I turned back, went and stayed with Uncle Stacy Grant in southwest part of Alliance. Next morning early I took the track again and overtook him in Smith Township, there I killed him and brought him back. That was in or about the year 1845.

Yours Respectfully,
Clayton Grant

BIOGRAPHY OF DR. JUDSON H. DAY[24]

For the interest of many persons have taken in furnishing data for the history of Lexington Township the thanks of the readers of the *Local* is hereby returned. Gratitude in this direction is laid under further contribution to Dr. Judson H.

---

[24] Originally published June 7, 21, & 28, 1873

Day, of Limaville, a life-long citizen of the township, for the following interesting paper.

The Dr., though in the practice of medicine near half a century of time, and near seventy years of age, is passing down life's declivity with an elastic step, erect figure, and apparently with the weight of not more than fifty years upon the vigor of his manhood. The Dr. has always enjoyed the fullest confidence of the people in his skilled care as physician. His practice has been extensive and his experience in the noble art of healing. As a physician he had seen one generation come and go, and the second generation pass all but its last mile post on the highway of time. May his coming years be many and set as lightly on his brow as those which have gone before.

———

– L. L. Lamborn, M. D. –

Dear Sir:

I have not done as well as I expected, not as you no doubt anticipated when you wrote me. My plea however, in extenuation of the seeming neglect in contributing my note to your very worthy effort in writing and publishing or preparing for publication the history of Lexington Township, is that since the reception of your note, I have been during most of the time better well to think of anything but myself, and when able to do anything at all, have been engaged professionally. And now, sir, in attempting to give you and the public an opportunity to look at my autobiography in a professional life, I shall expect you to give the facts that I may narrate such colorings and clothe them to the public eye, and shall prefer to have it all left out if you can supply in its place anything better.

The dates and facts are generally correct, and if they will aid you in your laudable enterprise I shall feel highly gratified.

I was born September 2nd, 1804, in the Township of Deerfield, Portage County, Ohio, about one mile east of the centre, and loved working on my father's farm until I was 21 years old; going to school in the winter and working on the farm during the summer. My father being only in moderate circumstances, I was compelled to learn all my mathematics in a common district school which at that early day was rather meager, so that much learning never made me mad. When I obtained my majority, I made choice of the practice of medicine for a livelihood and commenced my studies under the tutorship of Dr. John Menary of Deerfield, a man of excellent natural ability but uneducated. He was, however, a very successful practitioner of medicine, and a bold, intrepid surgeon, performing many operations of great danger with more than ordinary success. About six months after I commenced my studies with Dr. Menary, he was struck down with paralysis or hemiphlegia, of which he died some twelve or fifteen years after; this indisposition of course disqualified him for any kind of business. Dr. Thomas C. Shreve, a student of Dr. Benjamin Stanton of Salem, Ohio, having completed his studies, came to Deerfield and took Dr. Menary's place in the practice of medicine, and occupied his office. In the fall of 1826, I recommenced my studies under Dr. Thomas C. Shreve, and by him I was presented to the Board of Censors of the 18th Medical District of Ohio, and from that board I obtained my diploma, dated May 25th, 1830.

In the course of a week or two after I received my credentials, I was ready to embark in one of the most responsible duties belonging to human beings. I was in debt for my medicine, books, horse, saddle, bridle and saddlebags. I stuck my stake in Marlboro, one of the most enterprising places in the eastern part of Stark County at the time. The first return for professional services received after opening my office was 12 cents for medicine all in hard money. The next was a fee for extracting a tooth that was 12½ cents. The first obstinate case I was called to see was one of protracted labor of some four day's duration under the care of a midwife by the name of Mitts Fortune or skill in a very short time after my arrival I terminated the case favorably; and feeling a little jubilant over my success I manifested my joy by remarking that, "The job was jolted, the child was born, and its name was Anthony." The parents of the child, supposing that my name was Anthony, christened it "Anthony Day Yegly." This was my first namesake.

During the fall of 1831, I took up a temporary residence in Atwater Township for the purpose of teaching school in the winter following my practice not proving as lucrative as I desired, and accordingly I commenced my school about the first of December 1831, and taught three months. I think about the first of January 1832, a disease broke out in the south part of Marlboro Township, which was denominated lung fever. It was sub-acute in its character, and in but very few instances was there any fatal results although the length of time or course of fever was from four to six weeks, embracing whole families in some instances, while some escaped entirely.

I visited during that winter about thirty different patients, riding from Atwater after school on horseback and returning at hours varying from one or three o'clock the next morning. On one occasion I was so much exhausted for the want of sleep and so benumbed with cold that I fell from my horse into the snow, and came so near being frozen to death that had I been entirely from my bridle I should have remained there until taken away by some kind of hand. This was in February 1831.

The 28th of May 1832, I opened an office in Limaville, on Atwater Street, one door south of what was subsequently called Shillings' Corner, but up to that time I pitched my tent it was owned and occupied by a man by the name of John James. At this time there were six dwelling houses, one store, and one mill within the limits of what is now the Incorporated Village of Limaville. Peter Akey was the proprietor of the greater part of the village. David Holloway owned and occupied the lands on the north side of the village; a part of which was laid out in lots, and the remaining portion is now owned and occupied by Rev. Louis Paine. James Akey, father of Peter Akey, owned and occupied the lands bounding the east line of the village. Simon Dixon and his son John owned and occupied the lands south, and a widow Brown owned the land on the western border. John Grier was a prominent and enterprising farmer living a little distance west of the town and joining lands on the east with David Holloway. Mr. Grier was very worthy, extensively known, and highly appreciated in the township; the farm he owned and occupied was sold by him to Cyrus Oyster. In May 1833, George Gray came here and settled in a small frame house near the race bank; he and I are the oldest citizens now living in this place. John James opened the first dry goods store in 1832; his entire stock consisting of six pieces of calico, a few notions, some hardware, and a small quantity of groceries valued at about $150. Simon Dixon built the first sawmill in this vicinity near where the oil mill now stands. Lemuel Hawby built the first tannery in Limaville in 1832, and died about two years afterwards.

In 1835, I purchased of Peter Akey, the site upon which my house now stands, the place was called Rabbit Hill. It was at the time of purchase covered with large white oak trees and considerable underbrush such as hazelnut bushes, briers, etc. During the fall and winter of 1835, I succeeded in clearing off with my own hands all the timber and burning the brush, digging the most of them out root and branch. In the spring of 1837, I commenced building the house I now live in, and in the summer of 1838, (August 25th) was married to Susan L. Clark, of Buffalo, N. Y., by the Rev. Dr. Lord, of that city, and in October of that year I commenced keeping house.

Rabbit Hill

In 1839, I planted a row of black walnut trees in front of my house intended for shade or ornamental trees, the first of any kind that was planted in Limaville, but they were slow of growth, and did not live but one season, and I did not replant them, but in their stead I planted a row of sweet cherry trees, the first that were planted in the vicinity, they have flourished well bearing more or less fruit every year since they were three years old until the present season, only one of the number having died. In its place I planted the first soft maple ever transplanted in Limaville. In 1842, I planted the first grape vine, (an Isabella) which is still living, producing almost every year a sufficient quantity of fruit for the family and some to spare. In 1871, I expressed twenty gallons of wine from the fruit of that vine, using all we needed for the table besides.

In 1837, the first oil mill was erected in the Town of Limaville by Peter Akey, and after passing through many hands undergoing many alterations it is at present abandoned. In 1835, John C. Morse came to

Paine Home

Limaville with his family, and in 1838, he built a story and a half house on Church Street a little west of the northwest corner of Church and Adams Street, and attached to his house a small hatter's shop in which he worked for several years manufacturing with his own hands, I believe, the first hats manufactured in Lexington Township. The business not proving to be as lucrative as he anticipated or deserved he turned his attention to the study of law and in the course of a few years became quite a prominent advocate, his achievements were both honorable and profitable, leaving a better record when he moved from here in 1866, than very many others have left this place.

Rufus Paine came to Limaville in the spring of 1838, with his wife, one child, and considerable money capital, a part of which he had borrowed in the east at a small percentage. Mr. Paine bought the house and lot now owned and occupied by Mr. Muerman as a hotel, subsequently he purchased the property now occupied by his son, the Rev. Louis Paine, where he lived for a number of years; in 1859, he purchased a farm half a mile south of Limaville and lived there until he died. Mr. Paine accumulated considerable property by loaning money at exorbitant interests. He was eccentric in his interviews with the world, but temperate with his habits. The love of money absorbed almost every other consideration however he did occasionally give some of his money (Pharisaically), for the purpose of building churches, and in a few instances he gave to the poor and needy. He was a Quaker by birth and by faith — always using the plain language in conversation. His will was not an impartial and just one, but the disposition of his property was made equal by his son

Henry Paine to whom he had given the quarter part of it.

Epidemics[25]

In 1834, an epidemic of scarlet fever broke out in the southwest part of Lexington Township and the southeastern portion of Marlboro Township, of the anginose form. It was very severe in its character in a locality of two or three miles in circumference and was confined to what is called the headwaters of Little Bear Creek. Quite a number of families whom I visited were all lying prostrate at the same time, not one in the family being able to help themselves or one another even for a drink of water. There were but few deaths, however, if any. The treatment was red pepper gargle and warm water to the surface. Some thirty or forty cases were under treatment by me during that epidemic.

In 1835, another epidemic of scarlet fever and measles broke out in Williamsport, in the vicinity of what is now Alliance, the only instance I ever saw of the two diseases manifested in combination, and in this epidemic a number of persons died, both old and young. One elderly lady died while I was present; on my arrival at the house I informed the friends of the patient that she would die and immediately they set in motion the most enthusiastic praying and crying that I ever witnessed before or since. They got the patient out of the bed and formed a circle around her and commenced hallowing and praying to their God to save

---

[25] Originally published June 21 & 28, 1873

the patient. They kept it up for an hour or more when the lady became exhausted and fell, upon being raised to the bed she died in a very few minutes, so the prayer did not avail any more than medicine.

In 1842, an epidemic broke out one and one half miles west of Limaville at the upper mill on Deer Creek of scarlatina maligna. Quite a number of patients died both adults and children — three died in twenty-four hours after the first symptoms of the disease were ushered in. Those who died (on all that I saw) had no eruptions upon the skin; the disease manifested itself in the throat by excessive swelling, which terminated in gangrene. Those on whom the eruptions made its appearance generally recovered, although convalescence was very protracted.

In September 1846, an epidemic of pernicious fever broke out in Limaville and its vicinity, of the most appalling character of any diseases that ever visited this town or township — none recovered who had the third chill, and I am of the opinion that all who were attacked with it would have died had not the most potent treatment been instituted in anticipation. In anticipation of the danger, the subjects of this disease were all, without exception, I believe adults.

In the early part of the summer of 1846, a disease made its appearance in the south west corner of the township, on the head waters of Big Brush Creek, which was denominated at the time of its existence typhus fever, but I now believe from my recollection of symptoms was only an inflammatory sort of what is now called typhoid fever. While families were prostrated at the same time, presenting a scene in some instances truly appalling; the disease made its attack upon two brothers in the harvest field on the 21st day of June. They were working for a Mr. Smith, on the farm now owned by Robert Taylor. One of the young men got to the house without help, the other one was found crawling on his hands and knees in a state of mental derangement and remained in that condition for three weeks. They were both confined to one small bedroom where after three weeks of severe illness they slowly convalesced. In about one week from the time these young men were taken down, about thirty others were smitten with the same fever, the disease assuming a more malignant character in every subsequent attack until about the middle of August, when the case became milder, or we understood better how to treat them. Drs. Thomas, Hindman, Delamater, and myself were the only physicians who witnessed the scourge. Many heads of families died, and a few children. It took all, old and young indiscriminately.

In 1863, an epidemic of measles (Rubiola) broke out about three miles southwest of Alliance, and diphtheria accompanied a number of cases as a sequel and generally terminated fatally. These were the first cases I witnessed in the township.

In 1853, typhoid fever commenced its havoc on the citizens of Lexington Township near Alliance, and has prevailed more or less ever since, and many of our best citizens were removed by it from our society.

War of 1812[26]

My memory carries me back to 1812, when the British Lion was prowling about the northern border of our state and the militia were called out to defend our rights. My father being one of the number had made all the readiness the circumstances would permit by borrowing his father's old musket, powder, horn, and pouch. On the morning he was to start, my mother and her three children were standing around him and he was trying to adjust the bayonet (bagonett the Yankees called it); it being rusty and hard to get off he struck it with his hand on the underside of the shoulder and threw it up into the air a sufficient distance for it to reverse its position and it came down point foremost and stuck in the top of my youngest sister's head, and being so nearly balanced it remained there until it was taken out.

The reminiscences of youth are perhaps not apropos. I can recollect still further back than 1812; I can recollect of sitting in the lap of one of the Indians (Nickshaw) and playing with his hunting accoutrements, when only three years old. He was one of the number who remained in Deerfield until Daniel Diver was shot and who disappeared immediately after that transaction.

Yours,
J. H. D. [Dr. Judson H. Day]

———

---

[26] Originally published June 28, 1873

The health of Lexington Township, in early times, was unprecedented. Ague did not make its appearance until twenty-three years after its settlement; since then it has effectively scourged the citizens along the course of the Mahoning, but of late years the disease is abating, and in a few years, doubtless, a case of ague will be a curiosity. In 1833, an epidemic of scarlet fever passed over the northern and eastern sections of the township, but was not so genial or so fatal as it was through Columbiana County. In the fall of 1847, typhoid fever prevailed in the township.

RECOLLECTIONS OF DR. JUDSON H. DAY[27]

— The following is from Dr. Judson H. Day of Lima[ville]: —

At the age of twelve years I felt an inclination to do something that would yield me at least a boy's income and as the forest at that early stage of civilization was teeming with wild animals of almost every species indigenous to this climate, I borrowed or rather took a very large steel trap (as it was called) which belonged to my grandfather and commenced trapping for foxes; the gray and red foxes were sufficiently annoying to the farmers, by their frequent visits to their barn yard, to attract considerable attention and I accordingly undertook to interpose in the farmer's behalf. I used to set my trap in the cleared land close to the forest where the foxes made their day invades, and covered it up with chaff, and on the pan of it I would place some fine meat; but Reynard was cunning and would steal the bait every night without springing the trap. Not willing to be beat out by Mr. Fox, I made a slight improvement in the application of the force by which the trap would

---

[27] Originally published August 9, 1873

61

be sprung. And the next morning to my surprise and great joy I found my trap had walked off, and I remember well the excitement which I felt and the cogitations as to how I would succeed in killing my captive when I should overtake him as I followed the trail of the grappling hook.

But I had not proceeded far before to my very great chagrin I found my trap with only a small portion of the fox in its jaws. The trap was armed with spikes, and one of the spikes passed through the upper jaw of the fox just behind the incision teeth leaving in the jaw of the trap two common teeth and the entire upper lip back to the corners of the mouth and the entire scalp exclusive of the ears. The struggle must have been a hard one yet he escaped with his life; but so disfigured that he became a terror to the other foxes and they left the neighborhood never to return in any considerable numbers while I remained there.

The next enterprise was trapping for wolves and with an equal amount of success. I took the same trap and a dead sheep about one mile into the forest and near the bank of the Mahoning River, and carefully set and concealed it under leaves by the side of the carcass. The next morning I was early on the spot to again find that my trap had walked off not on so many feet, however, as on the former occasion, for following the trail of the grappling hook among the brush where it occasionally caught, I found that the unfortunate animal, whatever it might be, had used a set of excellent teeth in cutting off the roots and branches to disengage the hook.

One can scarcely imagine how much faster the heart would beat and how suspended be his respiration in pursuing what he supposed to be a monster wolf with no human arm to succor in case of an engagement or encounter with, perhaps a wolf, a bear, or panther. My recollection of the fear and suspense I endured while cautiously following the trail through the thick underbrush is as vivid today as if it had occurred but yesterday.

I continued the pursuit, however, for a considerable distance, meandering and circuitous in its course until within a few rods of the beginning, where the trail was lost on the ice, which at that place bridged over the entire river except about six feet in the middle where the current was so strong that it did not freeze and here my captive in attempting to drink, as I supposed, went to the bottom and was drowned. The next summer with the aid of a canoe, after paddling up and down in the vicinity, or as near the spot as I could recollect where I lost the trail, I found my trap and the bones of an animal of a large size supposed to be a catamount or wildcat and here ended my experience in trapping.

Ghost Story

In those early days I used to hunt coons in company of other boys. On one occasion, in company with a boy somewhat older than myself, we were returning home rather late and in the graveyard, which was but a short distance from my father's house. We saw on the top of a hill some ten rods in advance of us something, that to our frightened eyes was magnified to the size of a small building or a large covered wagon and it appeared to us, in the moonlight, as white as driven snow. The object was in motion and slowly moving towards the side of the street and near the graveyard, it disappeared and to us seemed to go into the ground, and from the time we saw it we advanced not one step forward nor backward nor spoke one word of encouragement or alarm.

We had with us three large faithful dogs upon which we placed our chief dependence in case of an emergency, but they were frightened too and to augment our fears and render our condition the more precarious, we thought that nothing but the supernatural could possibly scare our dogs. But the crisis must come, we could not get home without passing the spectral spot, and accordingly we summoned all our courage to the rescue and started forward and as we approached the place where we saw it disappear we again saw the same object rising, as it appeared to us, out of the ground and slowly but steadily advancing toward us. By this time we had reached a point of desperation and with our dogs in close proximity and ready for battle we sprang forward and uttered a kind of spasmodic command to Tiger to seize him and in a moment the mask was thrown off with a crash and to our astonished eye revealed a living man that was Jesse R. Grant, the father of President Grant. The mask was a large cowhide dried over a pole with the flesh side out and the glare of the moonlight upon it and magnified by a superstitious belief in ghosts, rendered it to us as white as a winding sheet. But notwithstanding the severity of the trial it has a salutary effect on my mind from that down to the present period of time my days and nights have been free from spectral sights.

CIVIL WAR ENLISTMENTS[28]

"When the war-drum throbs no longer,
and the battle flags are furled,
Is the Parliament of Man —
the federation of the world"

Alfred Lord Tennyson, Locksley Hall

In 1830, the people of Lexington Township were called upon to meet and muster near Louisville. None attended the call; they were fined and took their case to a court of appeal, held at Osnaburg, but were defended by Ellis N. Johnson, Sr., and discharged on the technical grounds of the officers commanding not having signed the call officially. In 1844, it is said there was a fine, well-equipped, and well-drilled volunteer company in the township under the Captaincy of Henry Chance, better known as "Buckeye Broadaxe."

It was left for 1860, to stir deeply the military spirit of the township. This city was the headquarters of the military district. Captain John F. Oliver was acting Provost Marshall, John C. Mong, now a Justice of the Peace of Sandy Township, Drs. Johnson and Armstrong of this place, and Adam Heldenbrand, now Probate Judge of Stark County, were his assistants. Dr. Whiting of Canton, was the Surgeon. The writer has found no task so difficult as that of obtaining facts for a suitable and systematic article on Lexington Township in the war of 1860-1864. About all that is at hand is that the enlistments from the township were chiefly in the 13th, 19th, 65th, 104th and 115th Regiments.

The township was drafted once, being deficient in its quota of three men on the call, Charles Kurtz, Noah Davis, and John

---

[28] Originally published May 10, 1873

Stough. Substitutes were found by the township for the two first persons, and none was needed for John Stough as he was never found. On one or two other calls for men the citizens had to hustle themselves right lively for substitutes to avoid it. The 19th Regiment enlisted its men on what is now known as the Fair Grounds but was then known as Camp Ford. General Beaty, now a resident of Jackson Township was Colonel, and Mr. Hollingsworth from Mahoning County was Lieutenant Colonel; Dr. F. Hurxstall of Massillon (deceased), was Surgeon; Levi L. Lamborn was Contract Surgeon until the commissioned Surgeon assumed his duties. The hospital of the Regiment was in the north wing of the Lamborn's residence. The number of patients in hospital during the regiment's sojourn at Camp Ford, about three months, averaged ten a day.

Among the residents of the township who were commissioned officers as Lieutenants and above that rank might be mentioned. Edward Scranton, now in the employ of the Pittsburgh, Fort Wayne & Chicago Railway, who entered the 65th Regiment as Private, and returned as a Captain. Benjamin Prescott, now in the employ of Coates, Gray & Co., entered the same Regiment as a Private and returned a Captain. Milo Torrence went out in the 115th as Lieutenant; William Elliott, now of the city, went out in the ranks of the 115th as a Private and returned a Lieutenant. Mr. McConnell went out with the same Regiment as Captain; A. J. Ware, of Lima, went in the same Regiment as Captain. Jackson A. Lucy received a commission as Colonel for the 115th Regiment from the township. Henry Ellison, now cashier of the First National Bank of Alliance, went out in this Regiment as Lieutenant, and returned as Adjutant. Dr. Johnson Armstrong, now in the book and stationery business in this city went out as a Private in the 65th Regiment and returned as Lieutenant. Thomas Hair, the present popular and efficient clerk in Dr. P. H. Barr's drug store in Alliance, filled the post of hospital Steward in the 115th Regiment. Henry Camp left Alliance in the 65th Regiment as Captain; Moses Shalters went out as Lieutenant of the 104th and returned as Captain; Doctor Isaac Young went with the 104th as Lieutenant and returned with his surgeon's commission; Dr. K. G. Thomas (deceased), was commissioned as Surgeon of the 115th and was with his regiment for a few months; Dr. R. P. Johnson, at present practicing in Alliance, was a commissioned surgeon, and was with one or more Regiments and had charge of the medical department of one or more military posts.

In 1863, General Kirby Smith, on the Confederate side, menaced Cincinnati. Governor David Tod, issued a proclamation calling on the minute men or "squirrel hunters," to report with such arms as they could command, at Cincinnati. In twenty-four hours after this call reached Alliance, one hundred and twenty-five men were ready to embark. The hurry was so great they did not organize the company until they reached Columbus. During a brief delay in the cars, they retired back of the depot buildings and elected Dr. Johnson Armstrong captain—Dr. Armstrong had seen service in the 65th Regiment. There were ten or fifteen thousand men in the state who responded to the Governor's call, and it is hard to conceive of a more motley and ill-disciplined group. One regiment of men who had seen service could have routed in a panic, the whole fifteen thousand; not but what there was in them a sufficient amount of natural heroism, but they had no advantage of drill or discipline; more than this they had no weapons in which they had confidence. Many of the "Fuzees" that went from Alliance had not been fired for years, and were incapable of being discharged for the want of such essential features as a tube, and in one or two instances a lock, but probably the call had the effect designed by the state officials, for Kirby Smith retired from menacing Cincinnati from the hills on the Covington side of the river, and the next that was heard of him, he was displaying his forces somewhere in Texas.

The Alliance Company left their town nearly bereft of the male population. The bulk of the vigorous men were already in the war, but they consigned their business to their wives and mothers; or, as Bob Toom be said, speaking of his country, be "nailed the flag of the Republic to the mast of the ship of state, and consigned the vessel to the God of Battles, the lightning, and the storm."

When Captain Armstrong's company reached Cincinnati, it was evening, they found the denizens of the city, who are naturally hospitable, now doubly so through fear of Smith, and through courtesy to those who proffered them their aid, the company was fed at one of the market houses, and then quartered in the commodious gymnasium. After remaining in the building a day or two, orders were received to take the cars to Anderson's Landing, four miles below the city, where it was understood a portion of Smith's army was crossing. That point was reached and a camp struck on the vine clad hills of the Ohio. The only engagements the company had was with the ripe and luscious fruit in the adjoining vineyards. In time the camp was raised and all the members of the brave band who held the Thermopylaen pass of Anderson's Ferry returned to the embrace of their bereaved families. Tod issued an engraved certificate of discharge to each member of the company. It represents a blind man trying to shoot a squirrel. These are framed and heirlooms now.

It is with pleasure that the names of John H. Hare and of Dr. J. L. Brenton, the first Surgeon of the 33rd O. V. I., and the latter of the 115th O. V. I. are added for the roster of efficient and prominent citizens from the Mount of twenty years ago.

Additional Civil War Soldiers[29]

Last week's chapter contained a list of citizens of Lexington Township who held commissions in the Civil War of 1860-1864. To that list should be added the names of Columbus Haines who was leader in the 19th regimental band. A. L. Jones, Esq., had a commission in the Ohio Cavalry. Col. Snyder enlisted from this township and returned with the commission of Lieutenant Colonel in the 13th Regiment; at the time of enlisting he was a clerk in the dry goods establishment of Ely & Shaffer. He has since deceased. I. N. Campbell entered the war as a Private from the employ of Pettit & Nixon and returned with a Captain's commission in the 115th Regiment. Governor [John Allen] Campbell of Wyoming left this township and the service of Pettit & Nixon, for the war in the 1st O. V. I., and returned with commission. For meritorious conduct he received his present honorable appointment. Mr. James McGarr, a druggist of this city enlisted a company and received a Captain's commission in the 13th Regiment O. V. I. Mr. McGarr was of feeble health and he resigned his position, sold his business to Dr. P. H. Barr, and resettled to Pittsburgh, where he died.

---

[29] Originally published May 10, 1873

John Columbus Haines and the 19th OVI Regimental Band

A number of prominent and excellent citizens of this township held responsible and honorable positions in the War of 1860-1864, but enlisted from other counties and states.

Major Cantine, Superintendent of the City Gas Company, and Colonel Hinsdil, an extensive dealer in lumber; both of these gentlemen entered the service from the State of Michigan.

Captain King, of the mercantile firm of King, Weikart & Warren, entered the service from Columbiana County as a Private and returned as Captain in the 25th O. V. I. Captain Joseph W. Gillespie, whose truculent pen makes the *Local* a power in the land, was a Mount Union boy of twenty years ago, and entered the service as Captain in the 100th Regiment, Indiana Volunteer Infantry. Phillip J. Wang, now successfully engaged in the harness and saddlery business in this city was

Captain in the 10th Regiment O. V. I. — enlisting from Stark County.

Captain Rolli entered the service in an independent cavalry company started from Chicago, Illinois

Colonel Thomas C. Morris was so closely identified with our city by location and interests that it is proper to mention his name. He entered the service in the 80th Regiment of O. V. I. as Captain, and was promoted to Lieutenant Colonel. He is now acting Sheriff of Columbiana County.

Col. L. R. Davis, now a citizen of this place, entered the service from Cuyahoga County, as Captain in the 7th Ohio Regiment and returned with a commission of Lieutenant Colonel of the 187th Regiment.

Commodities and Businesses

EARLY MILLS[30]

How strangely are the conveniences enjoyed today contrasted with those of the settlers of this township at the beginning of the present century; when it is remembered that Charles Hamlin, father-in-law to Shadrach Felts; Nathan Gaskill, father-in-law to Joshua Hamlin, residing now just west of Alliance, and other persons had to go to the mouth of the Little Beaver to get their grain converted to flour. Corn was brought down the Ohio in barges, from the Monongahela region, and landed at the Little Beaver. From this source the first settlers obtained their supplies until these 'openings' or 'clearings' would yield them a sufficiency.

It required three days to go to mill and bring home two bushels of corn meal on horseback. The next approximation of

---

[30] Originally published February 8 & 15, 1873

a flouring mill to these localities was one erected in the vicinity of New Lisbon. It only required two days to go and return from the mill. This mill was considered quite convenient, and supplied all further demands in the way of luxury for a number of years.

The next great move in the mill line, towards degeneracy upon the part of the vigorous pioneers of Lexington Township, was to have flouring machinery so luxuriously near to their cabin doors that they could visit it with their batch of corn and return in a single day. So to meet this volumptuous demand, a mill was erected on the waters of the Mahoning in Deerfield Township, Portage County, and long known as "Laughlin Mill." It was opened and run by the father of Harvey Laughlin, Esq., a citizen of this city.

A satiety of epicurean convenience was at last reached, but the cause of development and decay was at work as it always has been and always will be. It ran Rome and Greece from noble, vigorous men to voluptuous imbeciles, and both became the easy prey of hardy enemies, who were destined to run this, the same course, and leave the track open for successors. It was true at the advent of the "Laughlin Mills" the settlers of Lexington Township had not reached the epicurean sensuality of Romans, at the era of their greatest debauchery, but their yearnings were in that direction. Powdered diamonds could not be drunk, but linsey-woolsey trousers could be substituted for buckskin breeches. The aromatic fruits of the tropics were not of easy access, but a flouring mill run by water, with wooden gudgeons, and costing the enormous fortune of four or eight hundred dollars, could be built within a stone throw of their clapboard cabin doors. There was the sweeping current of the Mahoning made into a highway of commerce by legislative enactments, restless to revolve the ponderous machinery.

The first grist mill in Lexington Township was south of the town of Lexington on the river, it was built by Aaron Stratton; a sawmill was built in conjunction with the mill. It was on the latter mill that Job Holloway, son of the pioneer Amos Holloway, lost his life by the falling of a beam. Job Holloway was the father of Mrs. William Antram now living with her excellent husband on a finely cultivated farm immediately west of Mt. Union. Treble was the quantity of rain fell in early times that falls now. The Mahoning was subject to three or four frightful freshets every year, inundating all the bottom lands. The river restive of all first restraints upon its swollen waters, washed away the first enterprise of the kind attempted in the township.

The next mill built in the township was by Bryan Elliot, on the less angry and more generous waters of Deer Creek, about one mile west of the village of Limaville. The mill, though frequently repaired, has run continuously since its first erection.

In 1818, a grist and sawmill of some greater pretensions was built in Williamsport by Johnson and Pennock, on the Mahoning. The water being insufficient at times, steam was introduced. It is, at present in successful operation under the management of Kirk & Co. This mill had been successively owned by Thomas Grant, John Grant, John Miller, Michael Miller, C. Russell, Buckman & Co., and others whose names are not obtained. Mr. Burgett, formerly of Paris Township, erected about 1863, a steam grist mill in Alliance, which has run continuously under his management since it was first started. The Limaville mill, Kirk & Co's. "City Mills," and Burgett's Mill are the three flouring mills now in operation in Lexington Township. The proprietors of these mills are all fine citizens, and their respective brands of flour have a good reputation in the market.

An incident is related to illustrate the jollifications of the settlers. In 1818, at the opening of the Williamsport mill, John Meese, a hunter of considerable note, had a large and ferocious male bovine, which he had broke to be led and carry burdens. He ladened this bull with a bag of corn, rustically ornamented his horns, and mounting on his back one of his boys that could play the fife, and to its sprightly music he led the beast to the new mill with the first grist ever ground in Alliance.

Sawmills are more transitory in their lives than grist mills. Rolla Day built the first sawmill in Lexington Township on the Mahoning. A sawmill was connected with the Williamsport grist mill, one was built on Rockhillton Creek on the farm now owned by David Rockhill, one in Freedom east of the present steam mill, one in Limaville, one about one mile west of Limaville, one on Beech Creek in the neighborhood of John Taylors, one on Little Beech Creek in the settlement of David Minser, another in the Hively neighborhood on the adjoining lands owned by Jacob Lower, the ruins of one is seen on the small brook west of the Scranton farm north of Lexington. There have been from ten to twelve water sawmills built in the township, but none have been erected since 1840. The ruins of some of the above located mills are found on what are now not even rivulets, water scarcely passing by the ruined tail races of these former mills, in the wettest season.

Steam sawmills have supplanted water mills; there have been five of these mills in the township. One was built in Alliance by George Stroup in 1857, sold by him to Watson & Barnaby and now owned by the latter member of that firm. Another steam sawmill is located north of Strong & Lower's warehouse, one at or near Carr's Corners, and one on land owned by Mr. Greenshields, three and one half miles north-west of Alliance, and one west of Limaville. The era of sawmills of all kinds has about passed. In this township timber is comparatively scarce and indifferent for sawing purposes. Pine and hemlock are brought into the city from the Saginaw region and sold as low as the native timber of the township.

But little sawed timber was used or needed prior to the era of water sawmills. The first sawed lumber commanded a value equal to twenty-five cents per hundred feet from 1815 to 1820. It was worth fifty cents a hundred feet from this date till 1845, when it brought in trade at Canton from seventy-five cents to one dollar per hundred feet. After this period the rapid development of the country and the increase in manufacturing, the price of lumber in the township has gradually advanced till it has reached it present price, vis., $2 per hundred feet for hard wood, beech, sugar, elm, oak, etc.; white cucumber and poplar commanded at the mills from $2 to $2.50 per hundred feet. This is probably the maximum price which sawed lumber of the township will ever reach, for the reason that the quality is fast deteriorating and hemlock and pine are now imported by the lumber merchants, and sold at the quoted rates.

EARLY WOOLEN MILLS[31]

There have been three woolen mills in Lexington Township. One was built south of Lexington, on the Mahoning, by W. S. Miller; it was sold by him to one Snyder under whose management the enterprise failed. It was then purchased by Lawrence Alexander, under whose practical control it manufactured a variety of fabrics for clothing, as well as carded wool. This mill burned in 18—.

---

[31] Originally published March 1, 1873

Mr. Alexander removed to Canton and now owns and runs fine woolen mills in that city.

Another woolen mill was built in Limaville by William Hicklen and sold to Mahlon Allison and then purchased by Elias Hoover. During the administration of the above parties the mill was operated for the purpose for which it was built; but Mr. Hoover sold it to John Ware for a chair factory, and while occupied was burned.

The third and last mill of this description was built on the Freedom side of the Mahoning. The race is yet to be seen, about which a law suit was commenced at the time the mill was ready to go into operating which defeated the project and the machinery was moved to the northern part of Portage County.

CULTIVATED FRUITS[32]

Spring has come with a smile of blessing.
Kissing the earth with her soft, warm breath,
Till it blushes in flowers at her gentle caressing,
And wakes from the winter's dream of death
        Poem "Spring" as published in Atlantic Monthly, July 1860

The wild fruits of Lexington Township, were the data complete, would form an interesting chapter of itself. Wild plums were very common and of most excellent flavor. They were found most frequently along the bottom lands of the Mahoning, Beech Creek, Deer Creek and other streams of the township. Can some pomologist answer why this luscious wild fruit, now almost lost to this section, has not been domesticated?

---

[32] Originally published May 10 & 17, 1873

Crab apples—many trees yet standing—were quite plenty in early times. This intensely sour fruit was much used by the first settlers for preserving. The core was forced out, and the whole apple, less the centre, was used, and formed an excellent preserve.

Wild gooseberries, were common and were used by the settlers.

Sarvis berry trees were usual and furnished excellent fruit.

Elderberries were first brought into use for the table in 1826.

Blackberries and raspberries grew rapidly in all "openings" made in the primitive forest and yielded annually a luxuriant crop.

Strawberries of the wild variety were tolerable plenty, and of much finer flavor then the mammoth varieties now cultivated. On the southern border of the township a wild variety of this berry is found, of a white color, and excellent flavor. Tradition says that an old bachelor by the name of Lippincot brought the fruit from New Jersey, in 1810, from which introduction a large section has become seeded.

The township from its earliest settlement to the present time has furnished to the boys a plentiful supply of shell-bark hickory nuts, and white and black walnuts. Chestnuts have always been scarce.

The first two pear trees planted in Lexington Township were in 1820. The seed was brought from Jersey and planted in a sugar trough, where they germinated, from which they were transplanted to where they now stand, on the west side of Mr. David Rockhill's farm house on the west side of the city limits of Alliance. They are now stately trees with a bearing capacity of twenty-five bushels each, and have never failed to yield their annual supply of fruit since they came into bearing. They have never been grafted, but their quality of fruit has been excellent, approximating the size and flavor of a Bartlett. Fifty years have passed since their infancy was cradled in a sugar trough; they are apparently good for half a century more service. If these two trees would average ten bushel each per annum, which is a reasonable estimate, the aggregate of their product for fifty years would be 1,000 bushels.

The first quince bush in Lexington Township was planted by David Harmer, who owned ten acres of land west of the Town of Alliance, and the quince bush was planted and grew, as near as can be recollected, about the coal shaft in Haines' addition. It was the Orange variety of quince. This primitive quince has a number of progeny in the township. Mr. David Rockhill cut a scion from this parent stock, and it is now growing on his farm. The quinces from Mr. Rockhill's bush have taken premiums at agricultural fairs.

The only apricot tree in the township which had perfected fruit is owned by Jonathan Ridgeway Haines. It is very warmly located in an offset of his brick house, facing the southeast. The tree has yielded a few perfected specimens of fruit, which is a cross between a peach and a plum.

This township was admirably adapted to the growth and fruiting of the peach. The crop never failed prior to 1840. The first grafted peach tree in the township was owned by John Grant, and was called the "Morris White." It seems from tradition that the unbudded peaches grown in the township in early times were of excellent quality — almost equaling our present grafted varieties.

The first apple orchards set out in the township were those on the Gaskill farm, a little south of Lexington and one about one-half mile west of the Town of Lexington, and on the farm known as the Wilderson farm, a little west of the village. These orchards were set out in 1778-1779. The trees were obtained from Evans' Nursery, located just east of the Town of Salem. They were not grafted trees. Mr. Stephen Hamlin, an aged and respected citizen, yet living in the city, came into the township in the year 1807, from the State of Virginia. He informed the writer that all the fruit trees put out in the township prior to 1820, were natural, or ungrafted fruit, the grafting and budding of fruit trees beginning about this period. The old orchard now owned by Jonathan Ridgeway Haines was set out by John Grant, in the year 1812. They are grand old trees, some of them thirty-five feet high, and near seven feet in circumference and often yield as high as thirty bushels of apples to the tree in a season. The trees in the orchard are still vigorous and healthy, though seventy winters and as many returning springs have alternately bared their boughs of foliage and reclothed them in verdure.

This orchard was probably cultivated when the trees were quite young. Mr. Haines plowed it in 1848, since which time it has laid in sod; and it is his opinion that it is the only plowing the orchard has had in fifty years.

The Cabbage apple, Ashmore, Seek-No-Further, Winesap, Red Streak, Pennock, Sheep Nose, Grey Romanite, and Vandiver are the chief varieties this orchard now produces. It consists of forty trees. There was in this collection a Priestly apple tree, the first, last and only one in the township. It was blown down by a storm.

It is believed that there is no township in this immediate section of the state better supplied with fruit of all modern varieties than is Lexington Township. The soil seems well adapted to apples, pears, grapes, and plums. The latter fruit, however, meets here with its deadly enemy the curculio.

All the varieties of small fruits do well in the township. There is no one person giving them especial cultivation and attention, but a number of persons are producing a surplus for the market. Mr. Samuel Brooks has a clever plantation of raspberries, embracing several varieties — Blackcap, Doolittle, Red, and White Antwerp, Philadelphia, etc. Mr. William Scott has given some attention to strawberry, cultivating plants and berries for the market; the Wilson, Albany, and Triomph de Grand are probably considered the better varieties. Gooseberries flourish admirably. The English varieties such as Crown Bob and White Smith, yield their enormous berries profusely without being subjected to mildew, as they are in most sections. The American Seedlings and Meaghton Seedling are a much smaller berry, but are exempt from the mildew here and everywhere.

There are but few if any huckleberries in the township, yet they are found in the city market every year, obtained from those immense swamps in Marlboro and Lake Townships.

Blackberries, generally of the Lawton variety are raised in the township for home consumption and the remainder thrown on the market.

Blackberries, raspberries, and strawberries sell in the Alliance market in their season from 10 to 15 cents per quart; gooseberries from 5 to 10 cents per quart. Apples from 50 cents to $1.00 per bushel. Pears from $1.00 to $2.00 per bushel. Quinces from $2.00 to $3.00 per bushel. Plums from $2.00 to $3.00 per bushel. Peaches bring a variable price; they are obtained for this market chiefly from the high lands in Carroll and Columbiana Counties. Grapes bring from 6 to 18 cents per pound. Mr. George Lee of Washington Township, had furnished this market with a greater quantity of berries than any other one man.

This locality presents an opportunity rarely equaled for the location of a small fruit farm. The Pittsburgh and Cleveland markets are scarcely superior to Alliance for these products, and in case of a surplus those former markets are within two or three hours of the picking.

CULTIVATION OF GRAPES[33]

The history of grape culture in Lexington Township is a matter of growing interest with the people. The adaptability of the climate would be rationally inferred when it is remembered that the Lake Shore region and the Ohio River section have long since established their pre-eminent suitability for the culture of the vine. Lexington Township is near midway between those two regions. Again the native grape vine flourished extraordinarily in the soil of Lexington. The forests were full of these wild vines, a few of which can still be seen, inches in diameter and their remotest tendrils grappling with the topmost branches of the tallest forest trees.

There were but few grape vines planted prior to 1850. Job Johnson planted the first vine in the township a few years prior to the above date.

The Isabella and Catawba were the only variety planted for a number of years after the grape began to be introduced.

Time has demonstrated that the Catawba is not adapted to this section. The Hartford Prolific and Concord are the kind of grapes now preferred. A crop of these varieties including the Isabella is as certain as any other variety of fruit in the township.

---

[33] Originally published August 16, 1873

83

The grape needs an annual pruning, and it is only a few years since the proper system has been understood and adopted.

Mr. William Scott residing on Mt. Union Street is called upon to trim most of the grape vines in this section of the township.

There are a few families who interest themselves in fruit around their homes, who have from one to twenty vines on their premises, some have as high as two hundred vines.

The only instance in the township of a plantation of vines of sufficient dimensions to be dignified by the name of "vin yard" embraces two acres of land, surrounded by a thrifty Osage orange hedge, located west of Mt. Union Street and is owned by William Brinker. The vin yard for a year or two after it was planted was somewhat neglected, but is now in splendid order and will certainly yield its owner an ample return for the labor bestowed upon it.

Mr. William Brinker is a contractor and builder in the city of Alliance, but has an amateur love for the cultivation of grapes and all varieties of fruit. He understands and personally superintends the cultivation and pruning.

The plantation of vines are trained to stakes and pruned on the renewal system.

Mr. Jacob Rudy has in cultivation probably one thousand vines. Outside of the above parties, probably all other growers of grape train on trellises and trim on the spur system.

There are many other varieties of grape vines cultivated in the township than those named, but by amateurs and in a small way.

The Liana, Isabella, Delaware, Rodgers, Hybrede, Nortons, Virginia, etc., etc., are grown.

Capt. John F. Oliver, late Mayor of the City of Alliance, established, a few years ago, a house of the ordinary green house style some seventy-five feet long, located at the west end of Ely Street, for the purpose of propagating grape vines from cuttings. For several years he threw thousands of vines on the market. He has abandoned the business for the more dignified occupation of banking in the city of Steubenville, to which place he has recently removed.

Grapes sell in the Alliance market from 18 cents down to six cents per pound owing to the earliness of the ripened berry and the scarcity of the crop.

The cultivation of foreign varieties of grapes under glass is just beginning to be introduced in the west. Dr. Watson of Massillon, is the only person in Stark County who has thus grown grapes. He had met with full success. Mr. Fast of the firm of Ballard, Fast & Co., of Canton has a glass grapery and the vines are old enough to fruit this season. Levi L. Lamborn claims to have the best devised cold grapery in the state. It is eighty feet long by fifteen feet wide and has a capacity to yield a ton of grapes. He planted one year old vines in the spring of 1872, yet confidently expects a few specimen bunches this season.

He has constructed a cold grapery twenty feet long by nine feet wide without the stationary rafters, and on the following plan.

Fourteen hot-bed sash, 3x6, a double tier of which forms the roof, the back is ten feet high and the front two feet high. The back is weather-boarded up, barn fashion and slated, except opening in the front and rear such as are necessary for ventilation. A door is in each end; a purline supports the lapping ends of the tiers of sash.

Thirteen of these sash are used for hot-beds in the spring affording glass for forty feet of hot-bed, the season they are needed for the purpose, the glass is not necessary on the house, there place being supplied with boards six feet long excepting one sash which is retained and affords all the light necessary in the house, after they have served their purpose on the hot-beds they are removed to the grapery. In this manner hot-bed sash are utilized the whole year and serve two efficient purposes. There is no fruit more certain than grapes under glass, the protection afforded by the house obviates the extreme of cold and rendered fruitage certain. There are other uses a grapery is put to scarcely secondary to the production afforded by the vine.

Chickens will lay eggs all winter when properly fed under glass. If the grapery is convenient to the residence it cannot be equaled as a place to dry clothes. It will afford the family lettuce, onions, and water cress six weeks sooner than they can be grown outside. It will afford cabbage and tomato plants the same time ahead of outdoor sowing. Early varieties of peaches such as Halls early and Crawford early by cutting the top roots, the true principal of dwarfing, planted in boxes and kept in the grapery during the winter will yield profusely every year, magnificent fruit. As to the cost of a grapery on the latter plan, 14 sash will cost $17.50; 4 boxes of glass will cost $12.50; lumber six hundred feet $12.00; total cost of the grapery $41.00.

The labor necessary can be done by one with ordinary mechanical ability and is not estimated. This outlay of cash will afford any farmer or townsman a twenty foot grapery and glass for forty feet of hot-beds.

James Amerman, Esq., of Alliance, a gentleman with all the qualities of an amateur in horticulture and floriculture has built a grapery with ten sash making the length fifteen feet and in the spring can utilize the sash on thirty feet of hot-beds. His fifteen foot grapery will have the capacity for fourteen vines.

The varieties of foreign grapes planted in the township are the white and black Muscat, Chasselas, Muscat, and Sweetwater.

The instructions given in this chapter are a distraction from the original purpose of these articles. It has been done by request.

OHIO RIVER AND COMMERCE[34]

On the 25th of August, 1827, the Ohio Canal was opened to navigation through Massillon and a new commercial era began in this section of the state. A cash market was opened for wheat in Massillon, and there had never been a time since, that this staple would not realize a cash consideration to the producer, of some amount. It first brought forty cents per bushel on the opening of the canal.

From 1827 until 1853, constitutes another era in the commerce of the township, modified by the probability of obtaining cash for wheat, wool and a few other farm products, sufficient to pay taxes and supply the necessaries of life; but the system of "trade" and "trust" was the rule. Merchants trusted farmers for a year and then secured their pork, wool, or a horse for their bills. The first article would be cut up and cured by the merchants and then teamed to the Ohio River, chiefly to Wellsville as a point. The wool would be sacked and forwarded to the east by teams. The horses would be kept until ten or twenty were gathered and then the merchant would take them over the mountains, to Philadelphia, and

---

[34] Originally published August 9, 1873

realize a money consideration for them with which he would pay for his next year's supply of merchandise. It required four weeks for a merchant to make this trip to the east.

The price of horses between the above dates ranged from twenty-five to forty dollars. Cows ranged from four to eight dollars; sheep from twenty-five to fifty cents; oats from eight to fifty cents per bushel; wheat from thirty-five cents to one dollar per bushel; eggs from no value to six cents per dozen, but cash was not paid for these articles or any other farm products by merchants, as a rule. Farmers felt fortunate if they could get such trade off to the "store keepers" in exchange for their commodities.

In 1853, the Ohio & Pennsylvania Railroad reorganized and recapitalized in 1860, under the name of Pittsburgh, Fort Wayne & Chicago Railway, was finished, as was the Pittsburgh, Fort Wayne & Chicago Railway, and the revolution in the trade of Lexington Township, begun in 1827, by the opening of navigation of the Ohio Canal, was fully consummated. Land between these dates ranged from ten to twenty dollars per acre. After the latter date it steadily rose from the above mentioned figures to seventy-five and one hundred and twenty-five dollars per acre.

By reason of the railroads passing through this township in 1853, it was at once brought, by the motive power of steam, to within two hours of the majestic chain of northern lakes through which from Chicago to the Gulf of St. Lawrence, sweeps the mighty commerce of the north. The hopes and expectations of the founders of the Town of Lexington in 1805, were that it would be the navigable communication with the Gulf of Mexico, are within two hours of a fine realization to-day. The Ohio River is within one hour not however, as they hoped by the circuitous route of the Mahoning, to the north of the Little Beaver. Pittsburgh, the iron mart of the continent, was brought within three hours of the township; the great markets of Philadelphia and New York on the Atlantic sea board, are only eighteen and twenty hours distant. The great Pacific Railroad taps the commerce of Asia at San Francisco six days off; and the products of the Mongolean climates are from the west to the east as are products of Caucassian Europe from the east to the west, on the Great Trunk line of Railroad which passed through the township.

The market today offers and pays cash for the simplest products of the garden or farm. August 25, 1827, saw the first boat in the Ohio Canal. July 4, 1853, saw the first Engine on the Cleveland Railroad. These instrumentalities have worked wonders in equalizing the commerce of the continent. They reduced, in this township, such staples as salt from $12 to $2 per barrel; nails from 25 cents to 8 cents per pound; iron from 20 cents to 5 cents per pound; they have raised wheat from 25 cents to $2 per bushel; cows from $5 to $40; horses from $40 to $140; oats from 10 cents to 40 cents per bushel; etc.

COMMODITIES[35]

The population of Lexington Township in 1820, was 165, all enumerated. In 1830, it was 869; in 1840, 1,600. The value of personal property in 1853, was $122,806, with $31,968 of an increase over the previous year. The value of real estate in 1853, was $183,783, with $15,175 of an increase over the value of the same property the year before — there being three times more of an increase of real estate, than in any township in the county, save Canton and Perry.

In 1852, Lexington Township had 6,000 acres of wheat, which yielded 13,564 bushels. The same year was cut 506 acres of

---

[35] Originally published June 28, 1873

---

corn, which produced 15,627 bushels. The soil of Lexington Township is thin and clayey. White oak timber was the chief variety in the northeast corner; the other sections grow more poplar, maple, beech, chestnut, etc. The soil in the neighborhood of the Town of Lexington seemed originally quite productive, but from bad husbandry or a deficiency of the proper elements of a good soil, it must be regarded as the poorest in the county. In my opinion, the free use of lime would fertilize the soil.

Politics never caused much excitement in this township, until the log cabin and cider campaign of 1840, since which time there has been a sufficiency of zeal manifested on all election occasions.

The stores in the township in 1828, were Jacob Shilling, Limaville; Stephen Hamlin, Lexington; Akey & Culbertson, Limaville; Matthias Hester, Freedom; Job Johnson, Mt. Union. The price of products and fabrics in 1826, and the present time, in which they dealt, is as follows:

— — PRICES — —		
	Old Times	Now
Wheat, per bushel	$ 0.31	$ 1.50
Corn	.15	.40
Potatoes	.10	.60
Oats	.10	.35
Apples and peaches	no sale	.75
Eggs, per dozen	.03	.25
Butter, per pound	.05	.25
Pork	.02	.05
Beef	.02	.07
Hay, per ton	3.50	14.00
Cow	9.00	50.00
Oxen, per yoke	50.00	200.00
Sheep, per head	1.00	10.00
Farm hands, per month	9.00	25.00
Cutting wheat per acre	.25	—
Teaching school, per month	12.00	50.00
Mechanics per day	.00	3.00
Tea per lb.	2.50	1.50
Coffee	.40	.25
Pepper	.60	.35
Salt, per barrel	5.00	2.25
Shirting, per yard	.40	.16
Calico	.40	.12

It would seem that the farmers and mechanics have not much to complain in the changes that have occurred in the prices in Ohio during the past forty years.

Sixty-eight years have passed since Nathan Gaskill and Amos Holloway in this township, on the Mahoning, made a shed of boughs, placing under it their household goods, they dignified the rude structure with the name of "cabin" and sanctified it with the holy name of "home."

The population in 1805, including women and children, did not exceed ten — in 1873, it exceeds six thousand. Its stream of increasing humanity has had during the period trying commercial vicissitudes. It began subsisting on bear meat and corn dodgers; today the products of the globe are at its doors if money issues the command.

Prior to 1812, the little money which came into the possession of the settlers was obtained from the sales of furs, wild honey, and maple sugars. A financial crisis followed the War of 1812-1813 and money could not be obtained for any of the primitive productions of the township. Salt, tea, coffee, the spices, shirtings, and other articles almost necessary for life commanded money, and could not be obtained for trade.

The spinning wheel, hand wool cards, flax break — now known and seen only as fossils of the olden time were introduced. They yielded an excellent substitute for finer cotton and woolen fabrics, but other essentials could not be produced and the want of them produced actual suffering. Nothing that the townships could produce would command money. The legislature tried to relieve the urgent wants which was general over the state, by chartering banks, after which the general government inaugurated the National Banks which made all state enterprises of a secular kind, and the depreciated or worthless circulating paper added loss to want. The condition of things extended from 1813 to 1826-1827, as late as the latter period, wheat was hauled to Canton, Massillon, New Lisbon, and Akron, and sold for twenty-five cents a bushel, and wheat did not command cash at this price until about this period.

POST OFFICES[36]

The Town of Lexington had a tavern, a store, a Friends' Meeting House, and a school; it had the thrift and economy common to Quakers. It had an expected future, and besides these grand frontier privileges, it had a weekly post office and was the headquarters of news for a large adjacent district. Mt. Union had no post office for twenty years after one was established in Lexington. Freedom had none for nearly forty years thereafter.

The post office in Freedom was established in 1848. David G. Hester, our present excellent townsman, was the first appointed. He held the position eighteen months. The first mail to Alliance or Freedom brought one paper, "Ohio Repository" and one letter. The gross receipts for the first quarter were seventeen dollars. The position was responsible and the distributive labors of the office arduous, and David resigned and Robert T. Buck (deceased), the father of Dr. R. M. Buck, formerly a physician of this place, was his successor. Mr. Hester kept the post office at his then residence, facing the Central Union School grounds. Mr. Buck then owned and occupied the grounds now known as "Garrison's Garden" at which point he dealt out the installments of news for three months. Not relishing the duties of the position, he sought a resignation and a successor for three months more, when one turned up in the person of Thomas Beer, a Telegraph operator, occupying a room in the frame depot building since burned, located opposite the present brick depot. Mr. Beer was an ardent Democrat. He turned his attention to the law, moved to Bucyrus, Crawford Co., Ohio, and has gained some eminence in his profession and has been twice honored by the citizens of

---

[36] Originally published February 22, 1873

that county with a seat in the councils of the state. Mr. Beers' successor was Harvey Laughlin, Esq., who held the office during the last two years of Buchanan's administration. The post office during his term was in the building now occupied by J. Murray Webb, as a restaurant.

On the accession of Abraham Lincoln to the Presidency, David G. Hester was again appointed to the position of postmaster, and held the same for six years. A part of the time the office was in the building now occupied by Leek & McElroy as a provision store, and the balance of the time in the room now owned and used by Mr. Hester as a book and stationery store.

Mr. Hester yielded the post office to Wilson Culbertson through the persuasion of one Andrew Johnson. Mr. Culbertson located the office in the room now occupied by Dr. Fogle, as a drug store, his lease of office continued only six months when it was yielded to the Hon. Humphrey Hoover and returned to Mr. Hester's store. It continued under the management of Mr. Hoover for eighteen months.

Mr. Henry Shreve, an assistant in the office under Mr. Hoover, was his successor and had served the position of postmaster, acceptably to the departments and to the people for four years, and has been re-appointed and has entered probably upon another four-year lease. Mr. Shreve has had the office of Mr. James Vallilley's building on the west side of the Public Square. It requires three persons in the post office to discharge the labor. Mr. and Mrs. Shreve and "Kirky" are at present engaged in this duty; the latter is as genial and courteous as Henry is himself. It would be hard to find two more pleasant and affable public servants, than Henry Shreve and Kirk Allen. What better commentary on the development and growth of Lexington Township could be found, than the statement, that in 1848, the receipts of the post office at this point were seventeen dollars per quarter; now in 1873, they are over fifteen hundred dollars per quarter. The people of the township are further supplied with postal conveniences at Limaville and Mt. Union. The offices at these points may be referred to in a subsequent chapter.[37]

SCHOOLS[38]

"The education that forms the common mind,
Just as the twig is bent, the tree's inclined."

Alexander Pope

The first school ever opened in Lexington Township, was in the Town of Lexington, in the year 1809. The first school teacher in that school was Daniel Votaw. It was a subscription school, and under the management of the Society of Friends.

A few years thereafter a subscription school was opened in the vicinity of Limaville. The first school held in the Alliance section of the township, was held in a vacated cabin, on the land now owned by Clement Rockhill, just west of the Fair Grounds. It was taught by Andy Murran, in the year 1820.

It will be remembered that the present common school system of the state, was not instituted or organized until after 1824, consequently all schools prior to this date, were temporary, springing up in this or that locality, and living two or three months, as the school necessities of a neighborhood seemed to give them birth. They were held in vacated cabins and the teachers paid by subscription.

To Stark County belongs the credit of having sent a Representative to the State Legislature in 1822, who

---

[37] These locations were not mentioned in any other chapters.

[38] Originally published April 5, 1873

introduced the first bill which was ever introduced into the Legislature for the establishing and regulating of common schools in Ohio. I refer to Hon. James W. Lathrop, of Canton, an upright lawyer and Christian gentleman. The experience of almost half a century, has rendered changes in the law necessary, but to the Stark County Representative be the credit of having introduced a system of common schools that has, with its amendments, been found sufficiently comprehensive to educate all the children of the state. Every man who has lived in Stark County long enough to remember, and has noticed the current events can call to mind the opposition that

ALLIANCE UNION SCHOOL.

ESTABLISHED 1857.

burst upon Mr. Lathrop, on his return to his constituency. A howl went up against taxation and against Mr. Lathrop, but he was not to be driven from a righteous purpose. Knowing his law to be imperfect and having a well measured plan, he asked to be sent back, and was re-elected by a greatly reduced majority; he got his school law amended, increased the taxation for school purposes, and the howl increased. He was again a candidate and re-elected by a majority of less than fifty votes, but while at Columbus, in the winter of 1824, he died.

After 1824, and up to the time the union school system was adopted in Alliance, there was a small brick school house, 18 x 24, located in the immediate vicinity of the Disciple Church, which house was of sufficient capacity to meet all the educational wants of this locality. School was held in this small structure, three months every year. Since the establishment of the present school system, the township has been divided into ten separate school districts and each district has a neat and commodious school-house, with ample accommodations for the children of the district. In most of these districts a winter and summer school is taught.

School Superintendents

The union school of Alliance was organized under the act of February 21, 1849, in the month of February 1857. Mr. J. K. Pickett, was elected the first superintendent in March 1857, and continued to act in that capacity until January 1860.

George D. Hester was elected in August 1860, and continued until June 1861.

J. K. Pickett was re-elected April 1861, and continued until April 1865.

Jesse Markham was elected in March 1865, and continued until April 1865.

D. M. Miller was elected in April 1865, and continued until June 1866.

Ellis N. Johnson, Jr. was elected July 1866, and continued until June 1867.

W. H. Dressler was elected August 1867, and has continued to fill acceptably to the School Board and the people this very responsible position, from that time until the present.

The single building now known as the central school was all the school room afforded, or needed, as late as 1857.

In that year there were but 300 children in the Union School district.

The first Superintendent had four assistants. There are now thirteen assistants and the number of children of school age between 5 and 21 years of age, fifteen hundred.

The School Board has wisely adopted the distributive system of schools, locating one primary department in Webb's addition to the northeast section of the town, one on Market Street in the southwest section, one in Lamborn's addition in the southern section. The school board is now asking the voters to grant funds in the way of self-imposed tax to erect a fourth building to meet a growing want in the southeast section of the town.

The three primary departments already erected, are clever substantial two story brick structures, which have been built at a cost of about two thousand dollars each, to the people.

School-Age Children

The following official census report of the city of the number of youths between the age of 5 and 21 years, for the years 1867 and 1872 inclusive, also the number of children under five years of age for the year 1872:

1867. No. of children between 5 and 21 years of age, 610.
1868. No. of children between 5 and 21 years of age, 1,092.
1869. No. of children between 5 and 21 years of age, 1,128.
1870. No. of children between 5 and 21 years of age, 1,255.
1871. No. of children between 5 and 21 years of age, 1,393.
1872. No. of children between 5 and 21 years of age, 1,520.
1872. No. of children under 5 years of age, 698.

Mount Union College

The history of Lexington Township would be incomplete, should it fail to speak of an institution, which more than any other in the county, was humble and unpromising in its origin; yet, with objects based on the wants of the people, has overcome almost insurmountable obstacles, and stand, today, a source of usefulness, high in the confidence of the people of the county and the entire country. Mount Union College, first organized in 1846 as a small school with six pupils and a single teacher, was in 1858 regularly chartered under the laws of Ohio and of the United States, with full college and university powers, and a responsible and efficient Board of Trustees and faculty.

In addition to $75,000 donated in equal sums by Lewis Miller, C. Aultman and Jacob Miller for endowment purposes, important accessions have been lately made with the view of swelling the endowment to $300,000. The college grounds are beautiful, salubrious, and elevated 171 feet above the railroad station at Alliance, being distant two miles there from, and overlooking the Mahoning Valley and surrounding country. In the language of C. S. Porter, Architect, "The buildings of Mount Union College, are new, substantial, and commodious, are well furnished and finished; and containing the modern improvements are admirably adapted in all respects to College purposes."

Miller Hall and Chapman Hall on the Mount Union College campus

The College possesses an estimated property of a third of a million of dollars. The income from tuition, rents, and interest alone is over $20,000 a year. The College property is not owned as stock or individual property, but is held in trust by a Board of Trustees, elected by the patrons and donors of the property.

The Museum, unsurpassed by any other College, is of vast importance to students, as well as a source of popular instruction and entertainment to the public. Over $100,000 worth of specimens, obtained from all parts of the world, have lately been placed in this Museum.

About one third of the 8,310 students instructed at this College are ladies; also sustain about the same proportion to the 7,067 teachers trained in the Normal Department, who have taught public schools in nearly every state.

HISTORY OF NEWSPAPERS AND PRINTERS[39]

On Thursday, June 8th, 1854, the first newspaper was published in Lexington Township at Alliance. It was printed in Salem, Columbiana County, at the office of J. K. Rukenbrod, the present able and popular editor of the Salem *Republican*. Levi L. Lamborn, a practicing physician of Mt. Union was the editor.

A few weeks after this period a Washington Press and a tolerable printing office outfit was purchased of Lyman W. Hall, the present efficient editor and proprietor of the Portage County *Democrat*, and brought to Alliance and an office opened in Merchant's Block, in the room on the second floor immediately back of the rooms now occupied by A. L. Jones, Esq., as a law office.

After this, the paper was printed and published in Alliance. The paper was christened "The Alliance *Ledger*." By reference to the editorials of the *Ledger* recently reviewed, the fact was clearly elicited that the paper was strongly opposed to the Democratic Party. The readers of this article might infer this would be an astonishing disclosure to the author of the *History of Lexington Township*. The *Ledger* was also virulently anti-slavery and wonderfully Maine law-ish.

---

[39] Originally published April 26, 1873

After about one year's time, A. H. Lewis bought the entire interest in the *Ledger* and ran the paper for two years.

James Estell, Esq., then bought the office and ran a paper in the interest of the Democracy under the name of the *Times*. Mr. Estell removed from Alliance to Holmes County, Ohio, and published the Holmes County *Farmer*, and was elected Probate Judge of Holmes County, and received other evidence of the people's confidence and ability.

In 1856, Stuart G. McKee removed to Alliance from Carrolton, Carroll County, and purchased of Mr. Estell the *Times* office, and owned and published the paper under the name of the *Times* up to 1861.

Barlow & Morgan, Webb & Co., and Elmslie & Co., successively owned the office after this. Gotchell Bros. bought the office and moved it to Canton and published a paper there for a few months.

The *Democracy* of Alliance and surrounding country purchased the office and reshipped it to this city to print a paper under the management of one Robinson, who formerly had some reputation as a writer, having been connected with the Cincinnati *Enquirer*. At one time, Mr. Robinson, though a virulent Democrat, patriotically held the national debt created by the war, should be promptly paid, and that the most expeditious plan to liquidate the nation's liabilities, was the payment of internal revenue by an extravagant consumption of whiskey. He largely and liberally practiced on his theory and the paper died.

Patterson & McKee purchased the office and issued the *Local*. After a time Joseph W. Gillespie purchased to Patterson interest in the office, continuing the paper under the same name.

Mr. Gillespie soon became the exclusive owner of the office, but feeling that a Washington hand press and accompanying material, much of it quite old, could not be made to meet the necessities of the increasing patronage of an enterprising town fast merging into a city, sold the press and office, the history of which had been briefly traced since 1854, to Lacock & Co., of Salineville, to which place it was shipped a few months back and where it is probably entering on the vicissitudes of twenty year's experience, such as it passed in Ravenna and Alliance.

After Stuart G. McKee sold his interest in the *Local* to Gillespie, he purchased a splendid cylinder press and jobber, with corresponding and accompanying outfit, and issued a weekly called the *Telegraph*. The *Telegraph* apparently was well supported and entering a career of unusual prosperity, when one morning the citizens of Alliance were astonished with the report that Gillespie of the *Local* had bought out the *Telegraph*. The latter paper supported the interests of the Democratic Party and the *Local* was the organ of the Republican Party. The purchase gave the *Local* every facility for successfully competing with the *Monitor*. There was more material than could be advantageously used obtained by the purchase of the *Telegraph* office, and Dr. Lewis bought the hand press and some of the material of Mr. Gillespie, and in the fall of 1872, started the *True Press*. Mr. Lewis managed the *Press* for a few months and then disposed of his office to W. F. Hart, who still owns the office and issues the *Press*. Mr. Mossgrove assisted him as foreman and associate editor.

The *Monitor* was started by J. W. Garrison and J. Hudson, July 13, 1864. In October 1865, Mr. Hudson sold his interest in the office to Garrison. This establishment in 1864, was a new and splendid outfit, with steam presses and all title adjuncts. Mr. Garrison sold to office to A. W. Taylor, and moved to Massillon where he inaugurated the Massillon *American*. Mr.

Taylor soon found a purchaser for the *Monitor* in the person of W. K. Brown, who still owns the office and regularly issues the paper.

While Mr. Garrison owned the *Monitor* office he printed for one year the Christian *Standard* a religious paper in the interest of the Christian Church, and edited by Rev. Isaac Errett; the *Ledger* under the management of A. H. Lewis; published for one year the *Family & School Instructor*, a monthly of respectable size and appearance projected by the faculty and students of Mount Union College. Mr. Gillespie of the *Local* has published for one year the *Literary Advocate*, a monthly emanating from the same source.

Mr. Patterson, now the excellent foreman of the *Local* office and McKee's partner in the publication of that paper before Gillespie purchased his interest, ran for several years a job office in the building now owned and occupied by J. Murray Webb.

The Weaver Brothers also ran a job office in this city before they purchased the Minerva *Commercial*.

Mr. Stuart McKee, who has almost constantly connected with the press of this city since 1854, in connection with his son-in-law, now runs a tidy and excellent job office in Harrold's Block.

Journalism in Alliance

This includes, so far as memory now serves, the various printing and newspaper enterprises in this city.

There are three papers now published in Alliance, the *Local*, *Monitor*, and *True Press*; all three of these weekly periodicals are fine appearing journals, alike creditable to the city and to their managers.

The *Local* is a party organ, giving its influence to the tenets and policy of the Republican organization. The *Monitor* is a hybrid, it tries the circus feat of riding two horses named Prohibition and Republicanism. The *True Press* belongs to the neuter gender hermaphrodite, some think it faces toward the Democracy. The *Monitor* is chiefly edited by Mrs. Brown, a clever lady, fine writer and excellent itemizer. The *Local* is done up by Joe Gillespie. Few local items pass unchronicled in his paper. He is brief and decisive in his retorts and criticisms.

The *Local* cuts, the *Monitor* tears, and the *True Press* poultices; the *Local* pills, the *Monitor* gripes, and the *True Press* soothes. All of these papers are ambitious; the *Local* for party dominancy, the *Monitor* for money, and the *True Press* for that quiet which came to the waves of Galilee. Out of the sanctum the *Local* is affectionate, the *Monitor* courteous, and the *True Press* placid. The *Local* pointed, the *Monitor* general, and the *True Press* is neither. The *Local* shoots at the heart, the *Monitor* at the whole body, and the *True Press* shudders. The editor of the *Local* is obese and childless, the editor of the *True Press* is gaunt and wifeless, and the editress of the *Monitor* is lithe and guileless.

They are an inimitable trio. Concretely they are prismatic, resolving a ray of life's great duties into primordial elements even to the negation principles of light, with all the intermingling rainbow tints. Abstractly they are less ostentatious and gaudy. It is true the *Local*, *Monitor*, and *True Press* are not the *Tribune*, *Herald*, and *Times*, or the editors Greeley, Bennett, and Raymond, but they are respectable in their spheres and the City of Alliance is proud of them as editors and citizens. In the way of journalism, Alliance is the peer of any interior town in Ohio. These presses are the heralds of the city's future; for them to languish is for the city to die at heart; for merchants and manufacturers to give orders for printing to traveling rats to advertise competing town *felo de se* — it is suicide — it is a stone at the goose or geese that lay the golden eggs; it may not kill but it wounds them.

Journalism in Alliance is developed beyond its present capacity, and these enterprises, employing in the aggregate thirty hands, need the fostering influence of the city, till development opens up a competition less emergent than a race for life.

RAILROADS[40]

Alliance is built at the crossing of the Pittsburgh, Fort Wayne & Chicago Railway and the Cleveland & Pittsburgh Railroad; the former is a continuation of the great Pennsylvania Central, through Ohio, Indiana, and Illinois, to the city of Chicago; the latter connecting the "Forest" with the "Iron" city and with its branches associating in business relations with those two great inland marts a wide farming and grazing district in the Buckeye State. The etymology of the term denotes its origin, and though it has resulted that these two routes were not really allied at the time the town was named, but it was supposed they would be.

---

[40] Originally published July 5 & 12, 1873

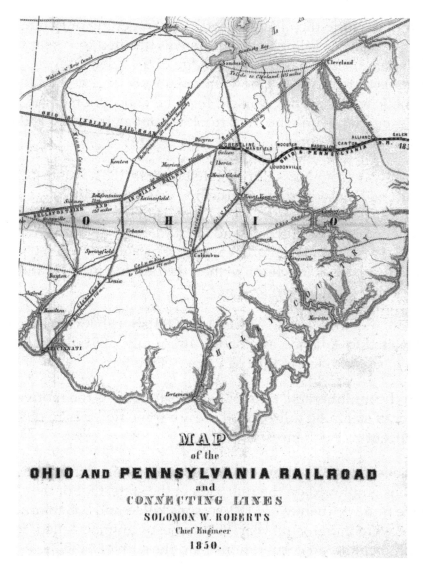

In 1831, a route was surveyed from Massillon to Pittsburgh, but the project was abandoned after an act of incorporation was obtained, because it was deemed impracticable to even attempt to climb the hills. The difficulty in getting over Buck Hill between Massillon and Canton was deemed too great to be obviated. Such was the knowledge of the science of railroads forty years ago; now they span a continent, and the magnetic telegraph has realized the wild conception of the Shakespearian hero who undertook to "put a girdle about the earth in forty minutes."

The railway from Massillon to Pittsburgh in 1831, was abandoned, notwithstanding the line was run by an accomplished graduate of West Point Military Academy, the late General O. M. Mitchell, and abandoned for the reason stated. The Pittsburgh, Fort Wayne & Chicago Railway is located on a track less feasible than the one run in 1831; and was projected sixteen years later.

In 1850, the grade of the Cleveland & Pittsburgh Railroad was completed to Alliance, and on the 4th of July, 1851, the first train of cars arrived in the old town of Freedom.

With the innumerable train of benefits following the motive power of steam on railroads, there are some reverses to the beneficent consequences.

The census of 1872, shows that in Ohio there are 25,393 persons employed on the railroads in the state. Out of the above number there were 192 persons killed and 358 injured. There were in the same year, 957 domestic animals killed, for which the railroad corporations paid the sum of $455.73.

Of the whole number employed on railroads in Ohio, in round numbers, eighty per cent are annually killed, and of the whole number employed fourteen per cent are annually wounded.[41]

---

[41]The actual percentage of people who were killed annually is 8%, not 80%

In well and evenly contested battles, the extreme numbers killed is from five to twenty per cent of the whole army; and the numbers injured or wounded from ten to twenty per cent of the whole army in action.

Time does not permit a list of mortality resulting from the potential agency of steam in this township since 1853, but the aggregate can only be reached by doubling the scores.

The freaks of the harnessed element of power which human sagacity cannot avert are often singular and anomalous.

In 1867, an engine was standing attached to a train taking wood a few rods below the site now occupied by the Alliance Rolling Mill. Daniel Parker, a brother-in-law to Mr. Mossholder, at present and for years past, engineer on the Cleveland & Pittsburgh Railroad, was the engineer, Jacob Reynolds was fireman and a Mr. Anderson, conductor. The engine blew out at the rear end of the boiler and made a complete revolution, the wheels of the engine lighting within a few inches of where they stood before the whirl, throwing her truck forward 150 feet and lifting herself high enough not to injure the stack. Mr. Anderson was struck on the head by a detached piece of the boiler and instantly killed. Mr. Reynolds had his thigh broken and the play of forces lodged him under the engine where he was found when the engine righted. He recovered from his injuries, to lose his life in the breaking down of a bridge by his engine some years later.

One of the most serious railroad accidents in this township, occurred on the 5th day of December 1856. In this causality there were nine persons killed and twenty wounded. There was rivalry between the Pittsburgh, Fort Wayne & Chicago Railway Company and the Cleveland & Pittsburgh Railroad Company. A full train on the former road was starting west, crossing the track of the Cleveland & Pittsburgh Railroad, when a train on this road came thundering north at a frightful speed, striking the westward train about midway, carrying the middle of the train with crushing force into the wooden station house, then located north of the Pittsburgh, Fort Wayne & Chicago Railway. Among the citizens of this place then killed was Dr. Smith and wife, Mr. Otterholt, Mr. Rudy, and Mr. McIntyre, son-in-law of Mr. Isaac Hartzell.

The first gentleman on the Pittsburgh, Fort Wayne & Chicago Railway, at this point, as station agent, was:

Thomas J. Nixon, who figure successfully as such for a number of years, when he was promoted to the position of Master of Transportation for the Western Division, where he served with credit until called to a higher position on the Great Eastern Railroad, which is one of the connecting links between Chicago and Cincinnati. Mr. Nixon was long a respected resident of this place, previously hailing from Pennsylvania, his native State.

Dr. A. Jackson, successor to Mr. Nixon, also held the position for some time, and afterwards operated as pay-master. His nativity was of Pennsylvania.

One of the darkest periods in the history of this road, was in the year 1858 — when freights and passage run light — when its finances run low — when it took the finest financiering to make both ends meet and to pay off its monthly liabilities.

James D. Makin, at this time — when even this station was reporting but a meager amount — when doubt and fear and anxiety prevailed, took hold of it and its arduous duties with a firm and determined hand and from its chaotic condition, harmonized and made all clear and satisfactory, and the affairs of the company flourished here under his management and care. When everything is smooth and working cheerfully and cozily, any medium rate business man can push affairs along; but to bring order out of confusion and errors confused, requires more than common ability and tact.

Charles H. Weller, proved himself a most reliable and prompt official, and promotion removed him to Crestline, where he remained until lately. He had charge of the company's immense cattle yards at Chicago.

L. M. Morris won many warm and appreciative friends. He remained some time giving satisfaction to the company, when he resigned to embark in a more lucrative business in Pittsburgh.

Samuel S. Shimp, his successor, a better man than whom is not in the employ of the road. Mr. Shimp has long been a resident of this city and bears the character of an honest, upright gentleman and has proved himself adequate to the discharge of the duties in the numerous positions he has been called upon to fill in our midst.

The labors of the agent at this post at present are very arduous, double those of any of his predecessors, yet he moves through them all smoothly, giving entire satisfaction to the company and holding the good will of the community and road attachés with whom he comes in contact. Mr. Shimp had held this post of labor and responsibility longer than any of his predecessors, and the company has no reason to change as long as he is willing to serve them.

The passenger conductors on this road will rate favorably, as a body of polite and efficient officials, with those of any road in the country. Among their number are a few extra and congenial spirits — gentlemen worthy of the greatest confidence and regard — gentlemen true to the brightest instincts of manhood and friendship. The following compose the entire passenger corps:

J. W. Scott, Richard Youngblood, William H. Line, Theodore Gray, William Peeples, G. W. Burnett, James Ailes, William Colburn, David Patterson.

First on the list is the name of Major F. Scott, who is the oldest conductor on the road. He is always pleasant, courteous and prompt in the discharge of his duty. He entered the service of this company shortly after it went into successful running order; for several years operated as freight conductor, and was promoted for his efficiency, to a passenger train, in which position he has given general satisfaction.

Next on the list stands the name of J. B. Boyer, who has long been associated with railroading in the different capacities of telegraph operator and conductor. In 1852, he commenced telegraphing in New Lisbon, Columbiana County, where he continued until the year 1854, when he entered the employ of the Pittsburgh, Fort Wayne & Chicago Railway Company, and immediately took charge of the office at Loudonville. He remained at the post some eighteen months, when he engaged with the Bellfontaine Railroad Company, where he remained until he came to Alliance, to enter the employ of the old company. He took charge of this telegraph office April 12th, 1858. In November 1861, he was appointed dispatcher.

The following named gentlemen have served as agents at Alliance, for the Cleveland & Pittsburgh Railroad Company, in the order in which they are named:

B. J. Wells, Linus Ely, Jesse Reeves, David G. Hester, D. F. Fast, John C. Cleland.

Mr. Cleland is at present occupying the position, and has filled it with efficiency about eight years. Previous to his taking this post of confidence and responsibility, he was acting as mail agent on the same road, in which capacity he served with honor and ability for a number of years. He is a good, prompt, and courteous official.

The gentlemen who have filled the position of baggage master on the Pittsburgh, Fort Wayne & Chicago Railway are as follows:

J. M. Filsha, James Ailes, William Grubb, Isaac Teeters.

The latter gentleman has held the position for over fifteen years.

Masters of transportation on the above road at this point, have been Fracker, Thomas J. Nixon, Bean, Bradley, Shem, Wiggins, and Williams.

The express agents have been Dr. Jackson, David Morse, George Muiford, W. K. Tidball and _____ Rice.

The names of engineers on passenger trains on the east end are David Peppard, Frank Burt, John Shaw, John Hess, John Vanwormer, _____ Conger, George Lowe.

The corps of engineers at present on the west end is as follows: Robert Jackson, Thomas Williams, Samuel King, Benjamin Jewett, Cyrus Ramsey, and H. Israel.

The original hotel erected by the Pittsburgh, Fort Wayne, & Chicago Railway, (then known as the Ohio & Pennsylvania,) at the crossing, was taken charge of by Col. Daniel Sourbeck on the 12th day of May 1852, and soon it became noted for famous meals throughout the length of these great thoroughfares and their connections. Col. Sourbeck came here at the solicitation of members of that company especially to take charge of their House. To the Sourbeck House Alliance owes greatly to her early fame; for the excellent manner in which the House had been managed in all its department from his installation therein, has caused it to be spoken of far and near, and always has it been associated with the name of Alliance. This, for instance, we have heard the enquiry, "Where is this Alliance and its famous Sourbeck House?" We have heard its praises sounded from the "Sunny South" to the extreme Northwest, and from there to the share of the Atlantic, and the name of Alliance was universally associated with the reputation of this fine House. In the fall of 1852, the company erected the neat frame building which stood on the north side of the track, and here the good qualities of this excellent house were made more marked and brilliant than ever. In 1864, this building burned down with all its offices and appendages, and Sourbeck was compelled to remove for a time into his old quarters, where he remained until the fine brick he now occupies was completed, which he took possession of on the 10th day of September 1866. The Colonel's first advent into hoteling was in 1835, thirty-three years ago, and he had been engaged in it, without intermission, ever since. He was connected with the dry goods trade some five or six years. He was born in Allen Township, Cumberland County, Pennsylvania.

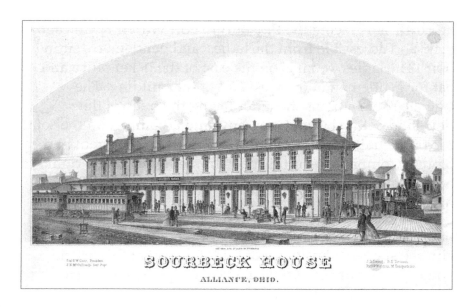

Sourbeck House

The fine brick hotel, in which he now presides, is superbly finished and arraigned, and furnished in a superior manner, with all the advantages of modern improvements and facilities. The building is 180 by 44 feet. The dining room 44 by 104. There are 25 fine, large bedrooms on the second floor. On the third floor are the rooms set apart for the attached, a large hall on the second floor extending the entire length of the building, eight feet wide.

On this floor is a large fine parlor also for the use of the lady guests. In the attic is a water tank, capable of holding about 50 barrel. This is used for cleansing purposes, generally, about the building. On the first floor, in addition to the dining room, is a hall running from the front of the building to the rear, north and south, dividing the offices and sitting rooms of the company from the dining hall. The offices and sitting rooms are in the west end of the building. The office of the hotel is on the south side, and the ticket office by the two companies on the north side, facing the Pittsburgh, Fort Wayne & Chicago track, and accessible from the ladies' and gentlemen's sitting room. The ladies' room is on the east of the ticket office and that for gentlemen in the west end of the building. The baggage room adjoins the latter facing the track of the Cleveland & Pittsburgh Company, and adjoining, on the south side of the building, is the office occupied by the agent of the Express Companies, for this post. Immediately to the right of the hall entrance from this side of the building is the hotel saloon.

Matt H. Robertson is so intimately and necessarily connected with the successful running of this House, that this article would be incomplete did we neglect to speak of him. He caters for the hotel, and most onerous are the duties thereof; yet he has proven himself thoroughly competent to the task.

No better man ever catered to the wants and appetites of man, than Matt. He has always the best on the table that a home and foreign market can afford and invariably served up in the best and richest style of the culinary art. Then there is George Vincent, one of the best of boys for the place he occupies — always prompt in the discharge of his duties as clerk — collects expeditiously and courteously, and is a favorite with all who visit this House, and their name is legion. George has occupied this position with the Colonel for twelve years. In the fall of 1861, he enlisted in the 10th Ohio Cavalry for the term of three years, and was one of the boys whose destiny it was to go with General Sherman to the ocean in the long marches, battles, skirmishes, etc. through Kentucky, Tennessee, Alabama, Georgia, and the Carolinas — part of the time as Private, Corporal and Orderly Sergeant. He may be ranked as one of "Sherman's Bummers," not through an ungentlemanly sense of the term, but as one of the boys who stood the blunt and fatigues of that awful campaign. All honor to him and the braves of that army. George was born in the town of Whimple, Devonshire, England, and came to this country in October 1858, then in his 17th year. At the time of his enlistment in the Union cause, he had held his present position four years, and eight since his return. His long service with the Colonel is the very best endorsement of his fitness for the position. With such attachés as we have named, added to the Colonel's over-seeing care and direction, all things run to perfection and in harmony.

Church Histories

Methodist Church[42]

As nearly as can now be ascertained, the first Methodist Society of Lexington Township was formed in the Village of Lexington, in 1819. It consisted of a class of six members of whom Thomas Wood was appointed leader. It was perhaps in the autumn of the same year that Lexington became a regular preaching stop, in connection with what was called Mahoning Circuit, with Calvin Ruttor and John Stewart, preachers. The Society first worshipped in private dwellings, then in an old school house. In 1827, they erected the first Methodist Episcopal Church built in the township. It was a rude affair, constructed of white oak, log puncheon seats, minus backs. In this homely structure they worshipped with slow but steady growth, until their present neat and comfortable building was erected. Some members of the first Society still survive, among

---

[42] Originally published July 19, 1873

119

these are Joshua Hamlin and wife. This venerable couple reside a short distance west of Alliance. They are quite infirm, but patiently awaiting the time of their release from earthly scenes. May their sun of life set in a cloudless sky.

In 1840, a class was formed and preaching was established in what was then called Williamsport, in connection with the Salem Circuit, Bro. M. L. Weekly, preacher in charge. The Society worshipped in private dwellings for a year or two, when they fixed up an old wheel-right shop for the purpose. In this extemporized church a series of meetings were held under the superintendence of the Rev. S. P. Kinear, which resulted in the conversion and addition to the church of about ninety persons. Among them was Henry Chance, the popular temperance lecturer known as the "Buckeye Broadaxe." Mr. Chance is still living and doing effective work in the cause of temperance.

This large addition to the Society, encouraged the hitherto little band to inaugurate a movement to secure, if possible, a house of their own in which to worship. The result was the erection of the frame building in which the Friends now hold service, located in what was called Freedom. Here the Society worshipped with constant growth, until 1865, when the house becoming too small for the congregation, it was sold about the first of May to the Society of Friends, who repaired and still occupy it as a place of worship. The congregation, then under the superintendence of Bro. A. B. Leonard, engaged in a new church enterprise which culminated in the erection of the brick building in which they now worship. This Society, now in 1873, has a membership of about four hundred, and which is constantly increasing.

The Sabbath school connected with the charge is one of the largest in Eastern Ohio. It is under the supervision of an able body of officers and teachers, and is in a flourishing condition.

The Society is under the charge of the Rev. W. H. Locke, their popular pastor, and just now is contemplating a radical improvement of their church building, which is greatly needed.

The truth is, Alliance ought to have better church accommodations and will no doubt, if the congregation of the Methodist Episcopal Church will undertake the erection of a first class church, they will have the earnest cooperation of the citizens generally, and will deserve the everlasting gratitude of everyone ambitious for the improvement of the growing young city of Alliance.

In 1841, a Society was formed and preaching established in Mt. Union by Rev. M. L. Weekly. This congregation had steadily prospered and is now in a flourishing condition.

Mt. Union, it is well known, is the seat of Mount Union College. It has unencumbered assets to the amount of three thousand dollars, and is constantly accumulating.

A Methodist Society has existed for years in Limaville. From a feeble start, it had grown into a vigorous band of Christian workers, numbering some fifty communicants, has a fine Sabbath school and a neat church.

There are now, in Lexington Township, about seven hundred members of the Methodist Episcopal Church, over eight hundred Sabbath school scholars, and over three hundred thousand dollars worth of church and college property. Besides all this a large number of the members of the church here, from time to time, moved to other sections of the country, while many have gone to the better land. This is but a brief and imperfect sketch of the Society of the Methodist Episcopal Church in Lexington Township. It is best we can do with our present limited data.

The following is a list of Methodist ministers who have served charged in Lexington Township and Alliance station since the church was organized, in the fall of 1839, with the dates of their respective appointments:

July 17, 1839..............Simon Elliot (deceased), M. L. Weekly
July 15, 1840..............Joseph Montgomery (transferred),
                            Thomas Thompson (deceased)
July 13, 1842..............G. D. Kinnear, J. Tribby
July 12, 1843..............J. Murry
July 10, [1844]...........J. Murry (located), Hosea McCall
July 2, 1845................Robert Wilkins (superannuated), Hosea
                            McCall, Henry Ambler (expelled)
July 1, 1846................David Hess, N. Gilmore (located)
June 30, 1847.............Hiram Gilmore (transferred),
                            James H. White (transferred)
July 5, 1847................John Huston, J. H. Rogers
June 1849...................Z. H. Gaston (superannuated)
June 1850...................Joshua Monroe (superannuated),
                            Richard Jordan
June 28, 1852.............Aaron H. Thomas (deceased),
                            John Ainsley
June 23, [1853]...........Hugh D. Fisher (transferred)
June 20, 1854.............Samuel Wakefield (superannuated)
June 13, 1855.............John Wright, Samuel Crow
June 1856...................J. C. High, S. Burt
April 28, 1857 ....Lewis J. Dales, E. D. Fast
April 29, 1858 ....David B. Campbell
April 27, 1859 ....M. S. Kendig, R. Morrow
March 20, 1861 ....A. E. Ward
March, 19, 1862 ....T. Storer
March 18, 1863 ....Wesley Smith, T. S. Hodgson
March 10, 1864 ....A. B. Leonard
March 15, 1865 ....John Williams
March 7, 1866 ....William Cox

March 18, 1868 ....W. K. Brown
March 17, 1869 ....George W. Johnson
March 15, 1871 ....S. P. Woolf
March 15, 1872 ....W. H. Locke

Of the above list, five have died, five are superannuated, three have located, six have been transferred to another conference, one expelled. Thus, out of forty-seven ministers, twenty-six only are in the work.

For many of the above facts we are indebted to the Rev. S. P. Woolf, late pastor of the Methodist Episcopal Church at this place.

Lutheran Church[43]

The first effort made to build up a Lutheran congregation in Alliance was in 1865, under the pastoral care of Rev. J. H. Brown. He organized with Dr. P. H. Barr, Peter D. Keplinger, Martin Tidd, William L. Kunkle, John Miller, Augustus Buckius, George H. Buckius, Emory Miller, and others. Judging from the records the enterprise began in a hopeful manner.

The Church Council (which is the official board of the congregation) were: Rev. J. H. Brown, pastor; Martin Tidd, William L. Kunkle, elders; George H. Buckius, Emory Miller, deacons, but for some reason failed.

The congregation owned no "House of Worship," which no doubt was to their disadvantage as well as a mistake.

---

[43] Originally published August 16, 1873

After the Rev. Mr. Brown resigned and left the field, the congregation had no regular pastor for over a year; when the Rev. A. Essic visited the congregation and endeavored to revive and continue the work, but it was too far gone for recovery. The members scattered; some by removal, some uniting with other churches, some losing interest in the work, whilst a few still entertained the hope for a Lutheran church.

The second undertaking, on the 4th of July 1872, Rev. J. L. Smith arrived in Alliance, under the auspices of the "Board of Home Missions of the Evangelical Lutheran Church," to begin the work anew. There was no Lutheran organization in the city at the time, as the previous one had disbanded. The missionary began his work at once by preaching, visiting Lutheran families and earnestly soliciting subscriptions for the erection of the church. He met with many difficulties by the way and the discouragements, arising from a previous failure, were hard to overcome. But with earnest resolve and indomitable perseverance, he went forward in the work. On the first of September 1872, he effected the organization of a new Lutheran Congregation, styled "The Evangelical Lutheran Church of the Holy Trinity," of Alliance, Ohio. A constitution and articles of discipline were adopted and officers regularly elected. On the 8th of September, one week after the organization was effected, the cornerstone for a church edifice was laid according to the liturgy services of the Lutheran Church in the presence of a very large audience. The pastor pushed the work forward as rapidly as possible, and the edifice was completed during the winter. The church is a fine Gothic structure, with tower, and beautifully furnished within, and cost six thousand dollars, not including the lot. It was dedicated on the 23rd of March 1873, and has no superior in the city for the beauty of situation and elegance of finish.

The enterprise met with much favor with many of the citizens. Too much credit cannot well be given to the little band of earnest men and women for the energy and self-denial by which they have made their work such a complete success. The whole work was done during the severest financial crisis the country has hereto felt, and yet the pastor and his church council have with united activity provided for five thousand dollars, leaving a debt of one thousand dollars to be met and collected. A Lutheran Church is now established in the city of Alliance, and as such commences its history.

The Church Council is Rev. J. L. Smith, pastor; W. D. Beeler, David Weikert, elders; Henry Miller, Peter D. Wonders, deacons.

The scats are free in the Trinity Lutheran Church, and the congregation is rejoicing with encouraging success. The congregation although not one year old until the first of September, has a new church finished, and a membership of over fifty. The Sunday school, lately organized, is hopefully growing, and the missionary feels greatly encouraged. Are there not some kind, generous friends who have as yet given no financial assistance, who will come forward and assist in liquidating the debt that is resting upon this young church? Let it be done in all kindness and trust.

The foregoing facts were obtained from the Rev. J. L. Smith, present pastor of the Evangelical Lutheran Church in Alliance.

Disciples of Christ Church[44]

In the year 1847, Levi Borton and family moved into the village of Mt. Union. A few days afterward M. D. Stallcup and family moved to the village. Mr. Borton, his wife, and one

---

[44] Originally published August 30 & September 5, 1873

daughter, M. D. Stallcup and wife were members of the Disciple Church. These five constituted the membership of this religious persuasion in the township in 1847. During the four years following this date by concert of action between Borton and Stallcup occasionally the services of this denomination were obtained at this point. Among the ministers who preached in the interests of the Disciples at this point during the period of four years might be mentioned: Israel Belton, John Whitacre (deceased), Benjamin Patterson (deceased), J. Warren, Joseph Moss, and J. H. Jones.

There was a small band of Baptists in Mt. Union, whose house of worship was obtained to hold the meetings called by those transient ministers. In March 1852, Mr. A. B. Green , accompanied by Austin Peter, of Warren, came to Mt. Union. Mr. Green preached sixteen discourses during this meeting.

Mrs. B. W. Johnson and others connected themselves with this persuasion during this meeting. There were at this time eight individuals banded together to investigate the scriptures and meet on the first day of every week. When steps towards and organization was taken the Baptists refused this little band the use of their house of worship.

They met together for two years in the old Seminary of the Peoples' meeting house. The members at this time consisted of Levi Borton, wife and daughter; Asa Silvers, M. D. Stallcup, and wife, Mrs. B. W. Johnson, and W. S. Pettit, at present an esteemed citizen of this city.

Mr. Benjamin Pigeon of Smith Township, recently deceased, associated himself with this organization. After the completion of the railroads through Alliance, this band changed their location to the Christian Church west of Alliance, at present used by Mr. Haines as a carriage house, and regularly organized, by appointing two deacons, and two elders, Asa Silvers and Bryan Patterson, elder, Edwin Vaughn and Edward Pettit, deacons.

Additions run the membership up at this time, to twenty members. About this time Mr. Harman Reves held a protracted meeting continuing for two weeks during which time there were some sixteen additions to the Church.

During the year of 1856, a series of protracted meetings were held at the Baptist Church, in old Freedom, since pulled down. One of these meetings was under the management of Mr. Dibble continuing some three weeks. The result of his efforts was the emersion of over forty persons. At this time father Hester, wife and two daughters connected themselves with this church. They were formerly Baptists. From 1847 to 1857, the church had no regular or continuous preaching. Levi Borton, Asa Silvers, and Benjamin Patterson officiated as ministers and instructor of the society in the absence of foreign presenters. Those three persons were the bone and sinew of this infant organization.

Father Silvers and Father Patterson are both gone to their rewards. They have left with hundreds whose eyes may fall upon these lines the full memory of a right legacy of being honest, pious, and true men. Mr. Borton is still with us firm in his primitive faith, and during the religious trials of thirty years had never faltered in the final triumphs of his faith, and in the successful establishment of a prosperous church in this neighborhood.

In the year 1857, the Disciples were yet without a house of worship in Alliance. They met in the old Baptist church owned by Matthias Hester who was then connected with the organization.

Elisha Teeters

Mr. Hester was born in Green County, Pennsylvania, in 1798. He came to Lexington Township in June 1838, and purchased sixty acres of land; part of which he still retains in the shape of town lots. After the Town of Freedom was laid out he erected his dwelling, and in August of the same year removed his family there. He has resided there since that time, and added several additions to the place, also erected a number of buildings.

At this time there was an octagon hall in the vicinity of Mr. Hester's present residence. This building was used for public purposes and on one occasion of a school exhibition, it was densely crowded and broke down killing one person and injuring several others. This hall was also used by the Disciples after the advent of A. B. Way to Alliance.

In 1858, steps were taken for the erection of a new meeting house. Mr. Hester furnished a lot and the building was erected, now occupied by this branch of the Christian Church. Mr. J. K. Picket, a number of years the superintendent of the Alliance Union School and Dr. Clover a physician succeeded Benjamin Patterson and Asa Silvers (deceased), in the eldership in the church.

Mr. Elisha Teeters, a member of the church, was about this time called to the eldership. Mr. Teeters was born in Green Township, Columbiana, Ohio, on the 11th of January 1814, and removed to this township in 1835.

Mr. Teeters laid out three additions to Alliance, respectively, in 1851, 1852, and 1853. The first addition surveyed by Ellis N. Johnson and the second and third by Mr. Whitacre. In these surveys Mr. Teeters carried the chain himself, and frequently joined in the chant of the professional carrier — "stick stuck" — over the fields and flats where now stands the City of Alliance. In 1852, lots were offered at public outcry by Mr.

Teeters, in his first addition; the lots upon which now stand the business blocks of Bleakly, Haines, Young and the private residences for some distance west along the north side of Main Street, were bid in for the proprietor at $40 a lot, that amount being considered too fabulous in the minds of the adventurous spirits present, ever to be realized again out of their sale. Some of these lots have since changed hands at $13,500 with but little improvements thereon.

Mr. Jehu B. Milner, a prominent citizen of Alliance, moved here from Salineville, Columbiana County, Ohio, was chosen an elder in the Church about this date.

Mr. Milner was born in Columbiana County, Ohio, in 1833. He is just in the prime of life, and we hope he may live long and enjoy his home.

The operations of Mr. Milner in our midst are somewhat extensive. He came to Alliance on the 15th of October 1863. The east wing of the Commercial Block was erected by him among his first efforts here. He laid out three additions to our city. The first addition contained 20 town lots; the second which comprises the old Nixon farm, where he now resides, contained 90; the third, that of the Garwood farm, contained 190; making three hundred lots in all which he has added to Alliance. He is a large contributor to the support of the Christian Church.

Mr. Pinkerton, a graduate of Bethany College, was called to the pastoral charge of the Church in 1866, and continued in charge for about two and a half years. Under his management, the Church was characterized by growth and prosperity, the membership amounting at this time to about one hundred and eighty.

Dr. R. P. Johnson, Samuel Milner, Isaac Jolly, Pliny Allen, and Horatus Hubbard were elected deacons of the Church in addition to Matthias Hester and others formerly mentioned.

Isaac Everett, President of the Alliance College, Profs. Benton, Hinsdale, and other members of the faculty of the College served the Church as ministers during the years following Mr. Pinkerton's administration. Mr. J. H. Jones followed and during one or more years was pastor of the Church.

W. S. Pettit who connected himself with the Church during boyhood in Mt. Union, was elected to the eldership about this time, also Amos W. Coates.

Mr. F. M. Green followed Mr. Jones in a year of pastoral labors for the Alliance Church. Mr. E. L. Frazier from Dayton, Ohio, is at present the efficient pastor of the Church and is in the second year of his labors.

Government

PUBLIC LANDS AND TAXATION[45]

In early times, from 1806 to 1812, taxes ranged from one to two dollars per section of land. The tax-gatherer annually traversed the township to collect this amount.

The taxes now levied and collected with the above period, are a grand commentary upon the enterprise and development of the country.

The Columbus correspondent of the Canton *Repository and Republican*, says that during the first administration of Washington, it was thought $600,000 would be necessary to carry the Government, and that Alexander Hamilton was the only man who seemed capable of devising ways and means to secure that amount of money. The population of the United States was then between three and four million. Stark County had a population of something over 58,000, and yet last year it paid in state, county, and local taxes, and in its proportionate

---

[45] Originally published April 12, 1873

share of federal taxes, $800,000 — $200,000 more than Washington's administration required its first year.

The readers of the *History of Lexington Township* will read with interest the following letter from Henry Cock, Esq.

Mr. Cock, some fifteen years back served the people of Stark County acceptably as Auditor. He is the son of Judge Cock (deceased), who represented the county in the legislature from Washington Township, and was the successor of Guy Kingsbury. More recently he served during the war as paymaster.

There's probably no man in the county more familiar with the detailed duties of the treasurer's and auditor's offices than Henry Cock, and during his career as public servant there has never been a charge against his integrity or honor.

> Dr. Lamborn, agreeably to a promise made at your bequest, I herewith hand you a statement of the taxes levied in Lexington Township. Also, an account of the public lands, of which its limits originally forms a part.

Public Lands

> The first public lands surveyed and laid out by the Government of the United States, in a regular and uniform manner, consisted of seven ranges, each six miles in width in the southeastern portion of Ohio, formerly known as the Steubenville Land District, and bounded as follows:

> Commencing on the right or north bank of the Ohio River, where it is intersected by the western boundary of the state of Pennsylvania, thence a base line was drawn westward forty-two miles, to the southwest

corner of Sandy Township, and a short distance west of the village of Magnolia. This point was also the northeast corner of the lands afterwards known as the U. S. Military District. From this point a meridian line was drawn southward to the Ohio River; and the lands lying east of this line and south of the first named line, as far east as the Ohio River constituted the Seven Ranges. Afterwards, the ranges were extended northward from the base line aforesaid, to the south line of the Connecticut Western Reserve, which is the north line of Lexington Township.

The Seven Ranges were surveyed in pursuance of an ordinance of Congress, passing May 20th, 1785, (before the adoption of the Constitution) and prescribing the mode of disposing of the public lands. Part of these lands were sold in New York in 1787. Other parts were sold in Philadelphia and Pittsburgh in 1796, and part was located under U. S. Military Land warrants; the act setting apart a portion of the state for the satisfaction of these military claims, not having then been passed. No further sale of land in the Seven Ranges took place until the opening of the Land Office in Steubenville, July 1, 1801. An act of Congress May 10th, 1800, created four such offices in the then territory of Ohio; viz., at Cincinnati, Chillicothe, Marietta, and Steubenville, the latter being opened as above stated.

The extension of the Seven Ranges northward to the Reserve Line was made in pursuance of an act of Congress, May 18th, 1796, as was also other lands lying westward of the Seven Ranges. These ranges were numbered westward from the Pennsylvania state line, and the townships into which the Seven Ranges were subdivided were numbered from the Ohio River northward to the Reserve Line. The Sixth Range, in which the civil Township of Lexington is situated, commences on the Ohio River at Newport, in Washington County, a short distance above Marietta, which Township No. 1, of Range No. 6, and terminates with Lexington Township, which is Township No. 19, of said range, and thus it is designated as an "original surveyed township." These ranges were sub-divided into townships, each six miles square, many of these however bordering on the river were not full, owing to its meanderings, and are called fractional townships, yet preserving their number.

All of the townships in the Sixth Range are fractional owing to a very singular occurrence. The surveyors employed to lay out the public lands under the act of May 1796, above referred to, divided the work, one taking one part and another the other. Commencing on the base line, on the north of the original Seven Ranges, as above described, they ran northward to the Reserve Line. One of these observing the true variation of the magnetic from the true meridian, whilst the other, made its variation in the wrong direction, i. e., to the left instead of to the right. The result was that in closing between the Sixth and Seventh Ranges a wedge-like tier of section is found, which instead of being the true width of one mile or 80 chains, is only 8.57 chains in width at the north end. This is the northwest corner of Lexington Township, and is 22.77 chains in width at the southwest corner. This, instead of being a full township of six miles square, Lexington is only a little more than five miles wide from east to west.

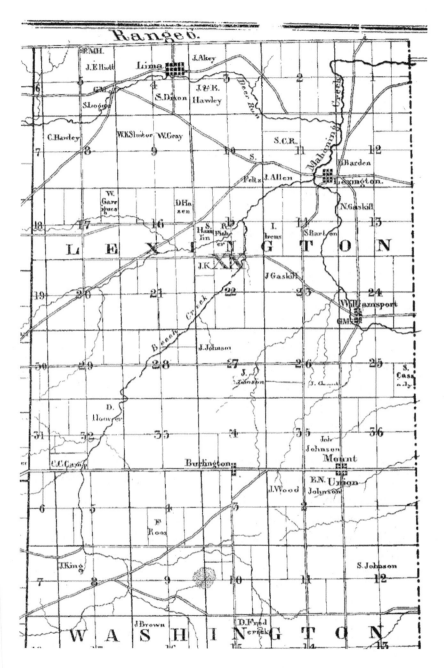

Portion of 1840 Map of Stark County,
compiled from authentic surveys by Lewis Vail

Original surveyed townships were sub-divided into sections of one mile square, or 640 acres — 36 sections in a full township. In the Seven Ranges south of the original base line, and also in the Marietta District sections were numbered in each township as follows; commencing in the southeast corner of the township with No. 1, thence northward to the northeast corner to No. 6, then dropping back to the south line west of No. 1 for No. 7 and so on, terminating at the northwest corner with No. 36. That part of these ranges lying north of said base line, however, including all the lands of Stark County, and all other public lands surveyed since that time are numbered differently. This is done by commencing in the northeast corner of a township with No. 1, thence westward to the west side, thence dropping down to the next row of sections and numbering back eastward, and so on backward and forward, terminating with section 36 in the southeast corner of each township. In this way the sections in Lexington are numbered sections 6, 7, 18, 19, 30 and 31 on the west side of the township being fractional for the reason before given.

Lexington Township was surveyed in December 1799, by Zaccheus Biggs and sub-divided in 1805, by William Heald, and was originally embraced within the limits of Columbiana County, which extended as far west as the Tuscarawas River and was bounded on the north by the Connecticut Western Reserve, and south by the U. S. Military District, being the south line of Pike and Sandy Townships. Stark County was established by legislative enactment in February 1808, and became organized as a separate county in January 1809; at which time it ceased to be a part of Columbiana County. Records of deeds, town plats etc., prior to that date will be found in New Lisbon. The original record of the plat of Canton is there, though all have since been transcribed into the record of Stark County.

The first county organization covering this part of Ohio was Washington County, established in 1788, extending from the Ohio to Lake Erie and as far southwest as the Sciota River. Next came Jefferson County in 1797; embracing the northern part of this territory. In March 1803, Columbiana County was established and afterwards Stark as above stated.

Taxation

I have experienced some trouble in arriving at a correct statement of the taxes assessed in Lexington Township. In fact no separate tax duplicate was made out for each township until 1826. Previous to that time the tax list for the entire county was made in one alphabetical list, and even since that date, the chain is broken. All the old books and papers have been twice removed within a few years past, viz., from the old office to the room in Wikidal's Block, and from thence to the new office after it was completed, and some are either lost or misplaced. I have not been able to find the duplicate of 1827, or an abstract of it. I find also that in 1839, the duplicate was not footed, or at least no additions are shown in it, neither can any abstract be found; I have estimated the amount however, from the valuation of 1838, and the rate of 1839, the result of which I give in the annexed table, which is complete with these exceptions. Though not precisely pertinent to the history of Lexington Township, I will here state that I find appended to the tax duplicate of 1823, the name of James W. Lathrop, Auditor of Stark County. He was afterwards elected to the State Legislature, and while in Columbus in attendance at the session of that body, sickened and died and was there buried; an account of which was recently published in the *Repository and Republican*, from the pen of our present worthy representative, Mr. Johnson.

The total amount of tax assessed on the duplicate of Stark County was in:

1820	$ 4,994.19	1823	$ 5,823.96
1821	4,181.85	1824	5,199.98
1822	4,125.77	1825	not found

In 1826, separate township lists were made, and the amount assessed upon Lexington Township was in:

1826	$ 132.64	1850	$ 2,096.07
1827	not found*46	1851	2,822.00
1828	237.64	1852	3,561.31
1829	264.26	1853	5,133.88
1830	284.23	1854	5,446.06
1831	343.02	1855	7,230.90
1832	439.19	1856	7,067.51
1833	444.87	1857	9,050,39
1834	394.06	1858	9,800.50
1835	375.35	1859	10,615.92
1836	565.68	1860	10,065.97
1837	898.87	1861	9,940.76
1838	850.43	1862	9,023.28

---

[46] Henry Cock, Esq., writes that he has found the tax duplicated of 1827 of Lexington Township, and the amount of tax assessed upon the township for that year was $185.72. This missing link makes the chain of tax duplicates for the township complete. [Footnote originally published in an Addenda from May 10, 1873]

1839 (estimated)..	908.95	1863	10,221.76
1840	1,020.26	1864	24,219.57
1841	1,251.50	1865	19,758.50
1842	1,271.38	1866	21,054.94
1843	1,351.46	1867	27,924.92
1844	1,284.93	1868	39,000.82
1845	1,326.96	1869	35,852.85
1846	1,547.96	1870	35,317.36
1847	1,843.90	1871	40,518.89
1848	1,908.58	1872	49,258.67
1849	1,852.15		

Making a grand total since 1826 of $415,781.07.

These amounts of course include Alliance, as well as the other portions of the township. No tax duplicate had been made for Alliance separately, except, that of 1872, when it was made in a separate list, and for the sake of convenience, will hereafter be so made.

Should you find the matter herein contained of sufficient interest to warrant its publication, you will please accept it as a contribution to the *History of Lexington Township.*

Respectfully,
H. COCK

LIMAVILLE GOVERNMENT[47]

The municipal government of Limaville was organized on April 3, 1841, by the election of Isaac Winans as Mayor. The

---

[47] Originally published June 28, 1873

following is a list of mayors elected by the citizens of the corporation since that time:

Isaac Winans ....April 30, 1841
Noah Upson.............no date
Northrup ....April 13, 1846
John Gallows............April 7, 1849
Arba Kidney.............April 9, 1951
Arba Kidney.............April 8, 1851
John G. Morse ....April 10, 1855
John G. Morse ....April 16, 1856
John G. Morse ....April 6, 1857
Stephen Logue ....April 4, 1859
Stephen Logue ....April 12, 1860
Mason H. Day ....April 1, 1861
E. B. Morse ....April 6, 1863
John G. Morse ....April 3, 1865
John G. Morse ....April 2, 1866
W. J. Osborn.............April 6, 1867
I. Ewan.....................April 6, 1868
W. E. Paxson ....April 6, 1869
W. E. Paxson ....April 8, 1870

JUSTICES OF THE PEACE (LEXINGTON)[48]

"Then the common sense of most will hold a fretful realm alive; then a kindly world will slumber"

Alfred Lord Tennyson, Lockley Hall[49]

For the following list of Justices of the Peace, the readers of the *History of Lexington Township* are indebted to the politeness of

---

[48] Originally published May 24 & 31, 1873
[49] Incorrectly attributed to Ross by Lamborn

Edward Page, Esq., at present the efficient and courteous clerk of the Common Pleas Court of Stark County.

Canton, Ohio. April 29, 1873

L.L. Lamborn, Esq.:

I herewith send you a list of Justices of the Peace in Lexington Township.

NAME	WHEN COMMISSIONED
Nathan Gaskill	May 19th, 1817
William Beeson	April 27th, 1820
Thomas Wood	April 27th, 1820
Thomas Wood	March 1st, 1823
John Wirmer	March 1st, 1823
John Greer	April 26th, 1826
Levi Burden	April 23rd, 1827
James Akey	May 1st, 1829
Levi Burden	April 24th, 1830
Thomas Wood	April 17th, 1832
Levi Burden	April 15th, 1833
Ellis N. Johnson	April 15th, 1833
Thomas Wood	April 23rd, 1835
Thomas Wright	April 16th, 1836
Joseph Johnson	April 28th, 1837
Mahlon Allison	April 17th, 1838
John D. Elliott	November 11th, 1839
Abraham Gaskill	April 29th, 1840
John G. Morse	November 23rd, 1840
John G. Morse	October 25th, 1843
Robert R. Barr	April 13th, 1846
Thomas J. Wood	October 30th, 1846
Talmadge W. Leek	April 22nd, 1847
Robert R. Barr	April 19th, 1849
Abraham Gaskill	July 28th, 1849

Thomas J. Wood ....October 20th, 1849
Robert M. Buck ....October 19th, 1852
A. L. Jones....................October 15th, 1856
Abraham Gaskill ....October 15th, 1856
John Ellison ....April 19th, 1856
B. B. Green....................October 15th, 1858
John G. Morse ....October 15th, 1858
John Ellison ....November 13th, 1860
John G. Morse ....October 12th, 1861
Joseph Barnaby.............November 9th, 1861
Joseph Barnaby.............October 14th, 1864
William C. Richmond ...October 14th, 1864
Joseph Barnaby.............October 18th, 1867
L. W. Loath....................October 18th, 1867
Simon Johnson.............February 18th, 1870
Jacob P. Zaizer ....October 28th, 1870
Joseph Barnaby.............March 20th, 1873

Jonathan Gaskill emigrated from Mt. Holly, New Jersey, to Lexington Township, in 1806. He raised a cabin on the farm between Alliance and Lexington now known by the location of the Gaskill Coal Bank. The force of men to raise the cabin was obtained from Salem, the nearest neighbors at that date. His son, Abraham Gaskill lived on a farm in the northwest part of the township. Nathan Gaskill belonged to the religious Society of Friends. He was the first Justice of the Peace of the township, in which capacity he served for three consecutive terms. Litigation was less frequent than now. During Nathan Gaskill's three official terms of office, he had before him but three cases for adjustment.

One was for a debt, the second was for slander, which was disposed of by the court decreeing that the parties should thereafter speak the truth or say nothing about each other. The third was an action of rape, brought by a married woman against her husband, which case was disposed of by friendly

admonitions of the court to the defendant to "be moc
all things."

During Nathan Gaskill's term of office he married two couples
all dressed in home-made linen. One groom was in his bare
feet and the bride had on a pair of stogie shoes but no
stockings.

Thomas Wood, Sr. came into Lexington Township in the year
1812, from the State of Virginia. He had five sons, Thomas,
James, Robert, Mathew, Calvin, and Daniel. The two latter
reside in Indiana, the mentioned first are deceased, Mrs.
Lorenzo Roath is a daughter of Thomas Wood, Sr. Mathew is
the only son now living in the township. Every citizen knows
Mathew; he has annually been elected assessor beyond which
the memory of the man runneth not.

Joshua Wood, one of the present commissioners of Stark
County, is a son of Robert Wood, and withal, a clever
gentleman and excellent citizen. Thomas was the third Justice
of the Peace elected in Lexington Township, and frequently
thereafter re-elected to the same office. The first law suit
before Thomas Wood, Sr. was "The State of Ohio vs. Benjamin
Gaskill." Said Gaskill lived just northwest of Alliance on the
place recently sold by George Zigler. The defendant was
charged with laziness and neglect of duty in the way of
supporting his family. The case was fully investigated and the
court discharged the defendant on the promise that he would
work eight hours per day in good weather thereafter, and that
he would quit running around and sponging his living off his
neighbors.

John Wirmer was the fourth Justice in the order of consecutive
election. One case brought before Mr. Wirmer was for breach
of contract. The Justice decided that the defendant should give
the plaintiff a pig at weaning time, make the clapboards as

soon as the weather would permit, and pay the costs of suit as soon as he could sell his maple sugar.

John Greer was the first Methodist class leader in the Methodist Church in the Limaville Circuit. He carried on the tanning business west of the Village of Limaville. His son, Joseph Greer, graduated at Meadville College, and is a presiding elder in the Methodist Church in the Erie Conference. Mr. John Greer, moved from Lexington into Trumbull County. He was in the order of election the sixth Magistrate of Lexington Township.

John D. Elliott was a brother-in-law to Mr. Greer, and was in order the seventeenth Justice of the Peace of this township. Mr. Elliott now lives in Logan County.

Mr. Levi Burden (deceased), was a son-in-law to the old pioneer Amos Holloway, a brother to David Burden (deceased), for a number of years prior to his death, a Justice in Smith Township, Mahoning County.

Levi Burden was the father of Amos Burden, a citizen of the township. He was in the order of election the eleventh Justice of the Peace of the township.

James Akey, the eighth Justice, lives now in Zanesville, Logan County, Ohio.

Mahlon Allison moved into this township from Salem, and was elected the sixteenth Justice of the Peace. He started a carding and woolen mill at Limaville. He left the township for Cuyahoga County.

Thomas Wright built the flouring mills yet known in Smith Township as Wright's Mills, from which locality he came to this township and was elected the fourteenth Justice. He owned the Saladay Addition to Alliance, and from the first house north of the Pittsburgh, Fort Wayne & Chicago Railway, he and his family moved to the state of Texas where he died; and also several members of his family deceased there. His widow returned and now resides in the township.

Ellis N. Johnson, Sr., was the twelfth in the line of commissioned Justices. He still resides on his farm where he settled in 1823, located on the western suburbs of Mt. Union. When Mr. Johnson was a magistrate, Lexington Township embraced all the territory of Washington Township.

John G. Morse, formerly a resident of Limaville, now of Dekora, Iowa, a lawyer by profession, was a courteous gentleman and excellent citizen. Notwithstanding his political convictions classed him with the minority party of the township, he was four times elected Justice of the Peace in Lexington Township.

Mr. B. B. Green, the thirty-third Justice of the township, lived in Limaville for a time was concerned in the pottery business. He now resides in Dekora, Iowa.

Joseph Johnson came to the township from Washington County, Pennsylvania, and settled in 1823, on the farm he now occupies west of Alliance. He was commissioned the fifteenth Magistrate of Lexington Township on April 28th, 1837.

Mr. Abraham Gaskill was the son of the first settler, Nathan Gaskill. He yet resides on a farm in the northwest corner of the township. Abraham Gaskill was three times elected Justice in Lexington Township. His first commission is dated April 26th, 1840.

Thomas J. Wood (deceased), was a son of Thomas Wood and a brother to Mathew Wood, the life assessor of Lexington Township. He was twice elected Justice of the Peace.

Jacob and Elizabeth Zaiser

Robert M. Buck (deceased), was a practicing physician. Though of the democratic politics, he was elected Justice in 1852.

A. L. Jones, Esq., a lawyer by profession, came to this township about 1850, from Columbiana County, and was commissioned Justice, October 16th, 1856. Mr. Jones still resides in this city practicing his profession.

John Ellison (deceased), came to this township from Marlboro. He was twice elected Justice. His widow and two daughters now reside in this city. Henry Ellison, the affable cashier of the First National Bank is a son of John Ellison.

William Beeson, Robert R. Barr, Talmadge W. Leek, William C. Richmond, L. W. Roach, Simon Johnson, have each discharged the highest judicial functions of the township.

Jacob P. Zaizer, at present one of the acting Justices of the township is a merchant and resides in Limaville.

There have been forty-two Justices of the Peace elected or commissioned in Lexington Township. Joseph Barnaby, the present acting Justice in the Alliance precinct, has been elected to the position three times. The first commission to Nathan Gaskill is dated May 19th, 1807, the last issued to Joseph Barnaby on March 29th, 1873; the interim embracing a period of over half a century of time.

FOUNDING OF ALLIANCE[50]

Alliance is the name given to the crossing of the Ohio & Pennsylvania and Cleveland & Pittsburgh Railroads. Alliance

---

[50] Originally published May 31, 1873

was named by Gen. Robinson (deceased), of Pittsburgh. The lots around the crossing were surveyed chiefly by the county surveyor, Mr. Whitacre, in 1851, and the proprietors of the adjoining land were Simeon Jennings, Joseph J. Brooks, Isaac N. Webb and Elisha Teeters.

Freedom lies upon the south side of the Mahoning, and was started about the year 1828, by Matthias Hester. The religious society that was first organized at Williamsport was of the Methodist faith; William Teeters and wife, and Perry Chance and wife, were among the first members.

And now that the town was located, it became necessary to improve it. Accordingly a house was built by Mr. Hester, the first house erected in Alliance and which is now standing, and occupied by Mr. Olliger. The same year Mr. Hester started a store, thereby being the first to establish mercantile pursuits in the town. Mr. Hester gave the town the name of Freedom by which it was known until ten or twelve years after its origin or until the completion of the Cleveland & Pittsburgh Railroad and Pittsburgh, Fort Wayne & Chicago Railway, when the railroad companies gave it the name of Alliance.

Mr. Hester made a public sale of lots, the same year in which the town was laid out, and disposed of several, upon which buildings were soon erected. In 1841, or about three years later Mr. Samuel Shaffer came here from Pennsylvania, and opened another store. Here was the first competition in trade in Alliance. And from these two insignificant establishments have sprung the 90 odd businesses of today. Verily, their progeny had been prolific.

For the first ten to twelve years, the growth of the town was very slow, the accessories were few and infrequent. Another store was added, a small brick school house, a church, and a few dwellings comprised the principal improvements. There was nothing here at this early day to attract immigration. The country was almost a wilderness. There was no milling privilege, there were few comforts of any kind to be obtained, and many annoyances and inconveniences were submitted to.

The post office was two or three miles distant. There were no markets for surplus products nearer than Massillon, 26 miles away, and to that point farmers would haul their grain receiving for it 40 or 50 cents per bushel. Our merchant's supplies were purchased at Pittsburgh and Philadelphia and transported by canal and river to Wellsville, and from thence by wagons to this place. In those days it required from four to six weeks, for our merchants to make the trip to Philadelphia, purchase goods and return. Now with our present railroad facilities, the same trip may be easily accomplished in the space of one week.

The ground upon which the city now stands was, at the time of the location of the town, owned by the following gentlemen: Matthias Hester, William Aultman, Michael and John Miller, Mr. Scott, and Mr. Cassiday. These gentlemen made numerous additions to the town, and public enterprises, in the way of land for the purpose of stimulating and encouraging the improvement of the town, but its progress was very tardy, and twelve years after its origin, or in the year 1850, the place contained only about 200 inhabitants.

ADDITIONS TO ALLIANCE[51]

Much the same that Altoona is on the east, Alliance is on the west of Pittsburgh, an offspring of the locomotive, a legitimate child of steam. In the history of the last few years a great chapter of which is occupied by railway events, an episode

---

[51] Originally published July 26, 1873

injected into the stale memoranda of former centuries which are continued in the stereotypes of diplomatic strategy, wars, marches, battles, and sieges this word Alliance has repeatedly appeared in the daily and weekly bulletins of news. Sometimes it has figured as the scene of unfortunate fatality, at others as the theatre of social or political demonstration, and the telegraph announcing to distant cities the arrival here, or the passage of this or that distinguished personage through the place, has helped to lend celebrity to the town.

The following is the [list of] additions to and composing the City of Alliance:

Matthias Hester and John Miller laid out the town of Freedom, July 24th, 1838, composed of 60 lots.

William Aultman laid out an addition to Freedom, September 17th, 1841, composed of 11 lots.

Matthias Hester laid out an addition to Freedom, September 17th, 1841, composed of 12 lots.

Alliance was laid out by Matthias Hester, September 10th, 1850, composed of 58 lots.

Elisha Teeters laid out an addition to Alliance, September 3rd, 1851, composed of 51 lots.

Matthias Hester laid out an addition to Alliance, September 10th, 1851, composed of 44 lots.

Jennings & Brooks laid out an addition to Alliance, May 21st, 1852, composed of 65 lots.

Isaac N. Webb, laid out an addition to Alliance, May 16th, 1852, composed of 16 lots.

William Teeters laid out an addition to Alliance, August 28th, 1852, composed of 8 lots.

Elisha Teeters laid out an addition to Alliance, May 29th, 1852, composed of 65 lots.

Samuel Shaffer laid out an addition to Alliance, April 15th, 1853, composed of 17 lots.

Matthias Hester laid out an addition to Alliance, December 13th, 1853, composed of 31 lots.

Elisha Teeters laid out an addition to Alliance, April 4th, 1855, composed of 37 lots.

John Miller laid out an addition to Freedom, July 3rd, 1856, composed of 7 lots.

Elisha Teeters laid out an addition to Alliance, June 14th, 1856, composed of 114 lots.

Isaac N. Webb laid out an addition to Alliance, May 27th, 1856, composed of 30 lots.

Isaac N. Webb laid out an addition to Alliance, June 9th, 1856, composed of 9 lots.

Matthias Hester laid out an addition to Alliance, February 27th, 1856, composed of 5 lots.

E. A. & C. W. laid out an addition to Alliance, July 7th, 1860, composed of − − lots.

Out lots 16.

Isaac N. Webb laid out an addition to Alliance, April 26th, 1861, composed of 9 lots.

Lee's out lots, laid out August 5th, 1863, composed of 24 lots.

Matthias Hester laid out an addition to Alliance, October 14th, 1856, composed of 14 lots.

Levi L. Lamborn, May 18th, 1866, and May 30th, 1868, composed of 152 lots.

Josiah Rosenberry laid out an addition to Alliance, June 5th, 1867, composed of 15 lots.

Jonathan Ridgeway Haines laid out an addition to Alliance, April 27th, 1864, composed of 28 lots.

Elisha Teeters laid out an addition to Alliance, December 19th, 1865, composed of 152 lots.

Linus Ely laid out an addition to Alliance, May 11th, 1870, composed of 6 lots.

G. W. Sears laid out an addition to Alliance, January 25th, 1870, composed of 17 lots.

Jehu B. Milner laid out an addition to Alliance, April 16th, 1866 composed of 20 lots.

Isaac N. Webb laid out an addition to Alliance, May 1st, 1866, composed of 25 lots.

Isaac N. Webb laid out an addition to Alliance, August 27th, 1866, composed of 32 lots.

Phillip Etiene laid out an addition to Alliance, July 29th, 1867, composed of 5 lots.

Elizabeth Grant laid out an addition to Alliance, November 14th, 1867, composed of 9 lots.

M. A. Ramsey laid out an addition to Alliance, June 14th, 1864, (out lots) composed of 12 lots.

Jonathan Ridgeway Haines laid out an addition to Alliance, June 29th, 1867, composed of 10 lots.

Grant & Rice laid out an addition to Alliance, July 13th, 1867, composed of 18 lots.

Matthias Hester laid out an addition to Alliance, December 18th, 1867, composed of 12 lots.

Moushey & Davis laid out an addition to Alliance, November 21st, 1867, composed of 6 lots.

Jehu B. Milner laid out an addition to Alliance, April 24th, 1868, composed of 205 lots.

Simon Johnson laid out an addition to Alliance, September 18th, 1868, composed of 13 lots.

Jehu B. Milner laid out an addition to Alliance, February 16th, 1867, composed of ?? lots.

Teeters, Lamborn & Co., laid out an addition to Alliance, various dates, composed of 990 lots.

Isaac N. Webb laid out an addition to Alliance, May 6th, 1870, composed of 24 lots.

B. F. Rosenberry laid out an addition to Alliance, November 20th, 1870, composed of 13 lots.

Buck's heirs laid out an addition to Alliance, March 13th, 1872, composed of 10 lots.

Isaac N. Webb laid out an addition to Alliance, February 22nd, 1870, composed of 11 lots.

Anna Webb laid out an addition to Alliance, May 14th, 1870, composed of 39 lots.

It will be seen that the city has 2,638 recorded lots. In addition to those are very many pieces of land but little larger than a lot, not numbered, upon which residences are built. There are 390 pieces of land upon the tax duplicate of the township outside of the incorporate limits of Alliance, Mt. Union, and Limaville.

The average amount of land to each land owner in the township is 39 acres.

The following is the [list of] additions and lots composing the Town of Limaville, to wit:

David Holloway laid out an addition to Limaville, December 8th, 1830, the same being composed of 10 lots.

Peter Akey, Isaac Winans, and Alva Proutz laid out an addition to Limaville, October 3rd, composed of 59 lots.

Peter Akey and A. Proutz laid out an addition to Limaville, July 24th, 1836, composed of 41 lots.

Thus Limaville has one hundred and thirty two recorded lots.

The following is the additions and lots composing the Town of Mt. Union, to wit:

Richard Fawcett laid out Mt. Union, August 22nd, 1838, the same at that date being composed of 30 lots.

John Hinds, Ellis N. Johnson, N. Hoiles, J. Watson, Rachel Hoiles, and Daniel Reeves laid out additions to Mt. Union composed of 30 lots.

Ellis N. Johnson laid out an addition to Mt. Union, May 22nd, 1851, composed of 4 lots.

J. B. York laid out an addition to Mt. Union, September 30th, 1863, composed of 45 lots.

Ellis N. Johnson laid out an addition to Mt. Union, November 29th, 1858, composed of 4 lots.

Pettit & Park laid out an addition to Mt. Union, March 29th, 1858, composed of 24 lots.

Jehu B. Milner laid out an addition to Mt. Union, July 20th, 1867, composed of 146 lots.

Ellis N. Johnson and J. P. Gould laid out an addition to Mt. Union, November 10th, 1871, composed of 10 lots.

This number added to the 390 pieces of land makes 3,447 distinct and separate pieces of real estate in Lexington Township. A number of lots are yet in the hands of the first owners, but probably not more than would be equaled by the pieces of land in the three incorporations which are not estimated in the above aggregate.

At a public sale of lots on Main Street in 1851, made by Mr. Elisha Teeters, the lots barely averaged $40 a piece. The lots known as the Reynold's corner was purchased by Mr. Jacob Oswalt of Washington Township at $37. He thought he had paid dear for his whistle, and got Mr. William Teeters, to take it off his hands. During the present year, 1873, the same lot with but little improvements on sold for $13,500.

It is to W. C. Wilcox, Esq., the affable Recorder of Stark County, we are indebted for a transcript, owners, and dates of the various additions to the township mentioned in this article.

ALLIANCE GOVERNMENT[52]

The present city government of Alliance (1873), is represented by the following officers:

> Mayor — Simon Johnson
> Clerk — A. W. Green
> Solicitor — William Pippitt
> Marshal — John C. Griffith
> Treasurer — William H. Teel
> Street Commissioner — Z. B. Johnson
> Council — B. F. Mercer, Henry Aultman, John McConnel, Joseph L. Brosius, John H. Sharer, Caleb Steele.
> Board of Health — L. R. Davis, William Stallcup, C. C. Douglas, Isaac Teeters, James C. Craven, Samuel S. Shimp.
> Health Officer — Dr. J. B. Wilson
> Policemen — Michael Condon, Solomon Berlin

---

[52] Originally published August 2, 1873

Mayors of Alliance[53]

There have been seventeen Mayors elected in Alliance since the city government was chartered on October 4, 1854, this being the date of the first Mayor's commission. The following are the names of past Mayors of Alliance.

Harvey Laughlin .... October 4, 1854
Harvey Laughlin .... April 4, 1855
Harvey Laughlin .... April 8, 1856
Harvey Laughlin .... April 11, 1857
Harvey Laughlin .... April 12, 1858
Linus Ely .... April 13, 1859
Simon Johnson .... April 4, 1860
Joseph Barnaby .... April 3, 1863
Joseph Barnaby .... April 3, 1864
A. L. Jones .... April 4, 1865
Henry Buck .... April 2, 1866
Henry Buck .... April 1, 1867
J. J. Parker .... April 5, 1869
Harvey Laughlin .... April 4, 1870
Harvey Laughlin .... April 6, 1871
John F. Oliver .... April 3, 1872
Simon Johnson .... April 7, 1873

The following are the receipts and expenditure of the corporation of Alliance, for each year since the organization of the municipal government of which minutes could be obtained.

Total receipts of 1855 ....$ 245.18
   "   expenditures..$ 60.16
   "   receipts of 1856....................................$ 232.77

---

[53] Originally published August 2, 1873

"	expenditures	$ 166.54
"	receipts of 1859	$ 308.58
"	expenditures	$ 302.34
"	receipts of 1860	$ 667.35
"	expenditures	$ 300.95
"	receipts of 1861	$ 791.25
"	expenditures	$ 357.99
"	receipts of 1862	$ 630.27
"	expenditures	$ 372.38
"	receipts of 1863	$1,291.55
"	expenditures	$ 718.22
"	receipts of 1867	$7,714.26
"	expenditures	$4,984.55
"	receipts of 1868	$9,924.63
"	expenditures	$6,126.88
"	receipts of 1869	$9,985.70
"	expenditures	$5,707.41
"	receipts of 1870	$12,199.63
"	expenditures	$11,626.93
"	receipts of 1871	$11,928.32
"	expenditures	$7,792.51
"	receipts of 1872	$18,584.80
"	expenditures	$12,367.51

The town house now in process of erection will be a substantial and creditable structure. It will endure and subserve its proposed purpose, for a half a century of time. A coming generation may be interested in the name of its builder and its cost. The following is appended. Some additions make the cost exceed $5,000.

The following proposals for building the town house were received:

J. T. Weybrecht ....$ 4,740.00
Baird, Aikin & Young.......................4,950.00
Ross & Robert Rue 5,400.00

J. T. Weybrecht being the lowest bidder the contract was awarded to him, and the building is to be finished in six months from date of contract.

Alliance's Town Hall

The following is the list of Recorders elected since the corporation of Alliance existed:

David Hoover, elected ....October 4, 1854
David G. Hester, elected .... April 2, 1855
David G. Hester, elected .... April 7, 1856
Jesse Reeves, appointed ....June 25, 1856
George McGuir, appointed.......October 17, 1856
George McGuir, elected .... April 7, 1857
Samuel S. Shimp, appointed ...... August 3, 1857
John C. Beer, elected .... April 2, 1858
David G. Hester, appointed ....May 17, 1858
David G. Hester, elected .... April 1, 1859
H. Camp, appointed ....December 12, 1859
David Hoover, elected.................... April 2, 1860
J. N. Ramsey, elected .... April 2, 1861
J. N. Ramsey, elected .... April 3, 1862
J. M. Culbertson, elected .... April 1863
J. M. Culbertson, elected .... April 1864
Peter D. Keplinger, elected .... April 1865
Joseph W. Barnaby, elected .... April 1866
Joseph W. Barnaby, appointed.......June 20, 1866
Joseph W. Barnaby, elected .... April 1867
Joseph W. Barnaby, elected .... April 1868
Joseph W. Barnaby, elected .... April 1869
Joseph W. Barnaby, elected .... April 1870
Joseph W. Barnaby, elected .... April 1871
A. W. Green, elected .... April 1872

The present efficient Clerk, A. W. Green, has assisted in furnishing of most of the above facts.

INDEX

Coates, Isaac, 27
Cock, Henry, 134
Colburn, Wm., 112
Cold grapery. *See* Greenhouses
Columbiana County, 138, 139
Commencements, 22
Commercial Block, 130
Condon, Michael, 157
Conger, 113
Conn, Edward, 22
Connecticut Western Reserve, 135
Cows, 88, 89
Cox, William, 122
Crab apples, 79
Craven, James C., 157
Crops
    Transporting, 73
Crossing, The, 106, 113, 149
Crow, Saumel, 122
Culbertson, J. M., 161
Culbertson, Wilson, 94

D

Dales, Lewis J., 122
Davis, L. R., 71, 157
Davis, Noah, 65
Day(?), Noah, 38
Day, Alva, 32, 35, 36
Day, John, 32
Day, Judson H., 50
Day, Mason H., 142
Day, Rolla, 76
De Grasse, Admiral, 29
Death by hanging, 29
Deer, 12, 49
Deer Creek, 9, 75
Deerfield, 18, 32, 38
Deerfield Township, 74
Delamater, Dr., 59
Democracy, 105
Dibble, Mr., 127
Dilworth, Joseph, 23, 25
Dinsmore, Isaac, 45
Diphtheria, 59
Diver, Daniel, 9, 60
Dixon, John, 53
Dixon, Simon, 53, 54

Douglas, C. C., 157
Dressler, W. H., 98

E

E. A. & C. W., 153
Edes, Lieut., 28
Eggs, 88
Egyptian mummies, 26
Elderberries, 79
Elliot, Bryan, 75
Elliot, Simon, 122
Elliott, John D., 143, 146
Elliott, Joseph, 48
Elliott, William, 66
Ellison, Henry, 66, 149
Ellison, John, 144, 149
Elmslie & Co., 102
Ely, 34
Ely, Linus, 33, 112, 154, 158
Ely, Merrick, 35, 36, 39
English, James, 26
Errett, Isaac, 104
Essic, A., 124
Estell, James, 102
Etiene, Phillip, 154
Evangelical Lutheran Church of the Holy
    Trinity, 124
Evangelical Lutheran Church, Board of
    Home Missions of the, 124
Evans' Nursery, 81
Everett, Isaac, 131
Ewan, I., 142

F

Fabrics, 92
Fair Grounds, 66
Farming, 5
Farnam, 33
Farnam, Judeth, 4
Fast, D. F., 112
Fast, E. D., 122
Fast, Mr., 85
Fawcett, Richard, 156
Felts, Jesse, 4
Felts, Shadrach, 4, 11, 73
Filsha, J. M., 113

Great squirrel hunt of 1832. *See* Squirrel
  hunts
Great Trunk line, 89
Green houses, 85
Green, A. B., 126
Green, A. W., 157, 161
Green, B. B., 144, 147
Green, F. M., 131
Green, General, 28
Greenshields, Mr., 76
Greer, John, 143, 146
Greer, Joseph, 146
Grier, John, 53
Griffith, John C., 157
Grimes, 34
Grubb, William, 113

H

Hadley, 34, 38
Haines Block, 130
Haines, Columbus, 69
Haines, Jonathan Ridgeway, 6, 13, 31,
  80, 81, 154
Hair, John, 21
Hair, Thomas, 66
Hall, Lyman W., 101
Hamilton, Alexander, 133
Hamlin, Charles, 73
Hamlin, E., 19
Hamlin, Joshua, 73, 120
Hamlin, Stephen, 81, 90
Hare, John H., 68
Harmer, David, 80
Harrold's Block, 104
Hart, W. F., 103
Hartzell, Isaac, 110
Hartzell, Josiah, 43
Hat manufacturing, 56
Hawby, Lemuel, 54
Hazen family, 16
Heald, William, 138
Heldenbrand, Adam, 65
Hess, David, 122
Hess, John, 113
Hester, David G., 93, 94, 112, 161
Hester, George D., 97

Hester, Matthias, 90, 127, 131, 150,
  151, 152, 153
Hicklen, William, 78
Hickory nuts, 79
High, J. C., 122
Hindman, Dr., 59
Hinds, John, 156
Hinsdale, Prof., 131
Hinsdil, Col., 70
Hodgson, T. S., 122
Hogs, 10
Hoiles, James, 17
Hoiles, Joseph, 22
Hoiles, N., 156
Hoiles, Rachel, 156
Hollingsworth, Mr., 66
Holloway, Amos, 7, 75, 91, 146
Holloway, David, 53, 155
Holloway, Job, 75
Honey, 13
Hoover, David, 161
Hoover, Elias, 78
Hoover, Humphrey, 5, 94
Horses, 87, 89
Hospitals, 66
Hotels, 113
Houses, 7
Hubbard family, 15
Hubbard, Horatus, 131
Huckleberries, 82
Hudson, J., 103
Hughes, Gideon, 7
Hunting, 16, 43
Hurxstall, F., 66
Huston, John, 122

I

Iron, 89
Israel, H., 113

J

Jackson, A., 110
Jackson, Dr., 113
Jackson, Robert, 113
James, John, 53
Jefferson County, 139

Lumber
Price of, 77
Lutheran Church. *See* Churches
Lutheran congregation, 123

M

Mace, John. *See* Meese, John
Mahoning Circuit, 119
Mahoning River, 5, 6, 9, 15, 17, 74, 75, 77
Main Street lots, 130
Makin, James D., 110
Maple sugar, 13
Markham, Jesse, 98
Massillon, 87
Massillon to Pittsburgh railroad route, 107
May, Charles, 15
Mayors of Alliance, 158
McCall, Hosea, 122
McConnel, John, 157
McConnell, Mr., 66
McGarr, James, 69
McGuir, George, 161
McIntyre, Mr., 110
McKee, Stuart G., 102, 103, 104
Measles, 57, 59
Meese, John, 12, 48, 76
Menary, John, 34, 35, 36, 51
Mercer Clearing, 17
Mercer, B. F., 157
Merchant's Block, 101
Methodist Church, 146, 150
Methodist ministers, 122
Methodist Society, 119
Miller, D. M., 98
Miller, Emory, 123
Miller, Henry, 125
Miller, Jacob, 99
Miller, John, 75, 123, 151, 152, 153
Miller, Lewis, 99
Miller, Michael, 75, 151
Miller, W. S., 77
Mills, 9, 74
Flour, 74
Flouring, 74
Grist, 75

Oil, 54, 55
Saw, 35, 54, 75
Steam, 76
Woolen, 77
Milner, Jehu B., 46, 130, 154, 155, 156
Milner, Samuel, 131
Milner's third addition, 46
Minser, David, 76
Mitchell, O. M., 108
Mong, John C., 65
Monroe, Joshua, 122
Montgomery, Joseph, 122
Morris, 17
Morris, L. M., 111
Morris, Thomas C., 71
Morrow, R., 122
Morse, David, 113
Morse, E. B., 142
Morse, John C., 55
Morse, John G., 142, 143, 144, 147
Moss, Joseph, 126
Mossgrove, Mr., 103
Mossholder, Mr., 109
Mount Union College, 99
Buildings, 100
Museum, 100
Publications, 104
Moushey & Davis addition, 154
Mt. Union, 18, 93, 121
Laying out lots in, 156
Muerman, Mr., 56
Muiford, George, 113
Mummies, 26
Murran, Andy, 95
Murry, J., 122
Muskrats, 10
Muster of 1830, 65

N

Nails, 89
Newspapers
Alliance *Ledger*, 101
Christian *Standard*, 104
Cincinnati *Enquirer*, 102
Democracy, 102
Family & School Instructor, 104
Holmes County *Farmer*, 102

Q

Quail, 12
Quinces, 80

R

Rabbit Hill, 54
Rabbits, 12
Raccoons, Hunting, 63
Railroad accidents, 109
Railroad casualties, 108
Railroad employees, 108
Ramsey, Cyrus, 113
Ramsey, J. N., 161
Ramsey, John Q., 47
Ramsey, M. A., 154
Rape case, 144
Raspberries, 79, 82
Rattlesnakes, 13
Receipts and expenditure of Alliance, 158
Recorders of Alliance, 161
Reeves, Daniel, 156
Reeves, Jesse, 112, 161
Republican organization, 105
Reves, Harman, 127
Revolutionary War, 28
Reynold's corner, 157
Reynolds, Jacob, 109
Rice, 113
Richmond, William C., 144, 149
Roach, L. W., 149
Roads, 3
Roath, Lorenzo, Mrs., 145
Robertson, Matt H., 116
Robinson, Gen., 150
Robinson, Mr., 102
Rockhill, Clement, 47, 48, 95
Rockhill, David, 31, 76, 79, 80
Rockhill, Nancy, 47
Rockhillton Creek, 76
Rogers, J. H., 122
Rolli, Captain, 71
Roofs, 20
Rosenberry, B. F., 155
Rosenberry, Josiah, 154
Ross & Robert Rue, 160

Rubiola, 59
Rudy, Jacob, 84
Rudy, Mr., 110
Rukenbrod, J. K., 101
Russell, C., 75
Ruttor, Calvin, 119

S

Sabbath school, 120
Sage's mill, 48
Saladay Addition, 146
Salem Circuit, 120
Salt, 17, 89
Sarvis berry, 79
Sawmills. *See* Mills:Saw
Saxton, John, 5
Scarlatina maligna, 58
Scarlet fever, 57, 61
School Board, 98
School Superintendents, 98
School system, Common, 95
School, Subscription, 95
Scott, F., 112
Scott, J. W., 112
Scott, Mr., 151
Scott, William, 82, 84
Scranton, Edward, 66
Sears, G. W., 154
Seven ranges, 134
Shaffer, Samuel, 150, 153
Shalters, Moses, 67
Sharer, John H., 157
Shaw, John, 113
Sheep, 33, 88
Shem, 113
Sherman's Bummers, 116
Shilling, Jacob, 90
Shillings' Corner, 53
Shimp, Samuel S., 111, 157, 161
Shirtz, James, 6
Shreve, Benjamin, 27
Shreve, Eliza, 27
Shreve, Henry, 27, 94
Shreve, Israel, 27
Shreve, John, 26, 27
Shreve, Joseph, 25, 26
Shreve, Mary, 27

War encounters, 4
War of 1812, 5, 8
Ward, A. E., 122
Ware, A. J., 66
Ware, John, 78
Warren, J., 126
Washington County, 139
Washington Township, 147
Washington, George, 29
Watson & Barnaby, 76
Watson, Dr., 85
Watson, J., 156
Way, A. B., 129
Weaver Brothers, 104
Webb & Co., 102
Webb, Anna, 155
Webb, Isaac N., 150, 152
Webb, J. Murray, 94, 104
Webb, Richard, 21
Webb's addition, 98
Weekly, M. L., 120, 121, 122
Weikert, David, 125
Weller, Charles H., 111
Wells, B. J., 112
Wellsville, 87
Western Reserve line, 135
Weybrecht, J. T., 160
Wheat, 5, 46, 87, 88, 89, 92
Wheat Sickness, 46
Whitacre, John, 126, 129, 150
White, James H., 122
Whiting, Dr., 65
Wiggins, 113
Wikidal's Block, 139
Wilcox, W. C., 157
Wilderson farm, 81
Wilkins, Robert, 122
Williams, 113

Williams, John, 122
Williams, Thomas, 113
Williamsport, 18, 75, 120, 150
Wilson, J. B., 157
Winans, Isaac, 141, 142, 156
Windows, 21
Wirmer, John, 143, 145
Wolves, 12, 15, 62
Wonders, Peter D., 125
Wood, Calvin, 145
Wood, Daniel, 145
Wood, James, 145
Wood, Joshua, 145
Wood, Mathew, 145, 147
Wood, Robert, 145
Wood, Thomas, 119, 143, 147
Wood, Thomas J., 143, 147
Wood, Thomas, Sr., 145
Woodruff, Dr., 25
Wool, 33, 87
Woolf, S. P., 123
Wright, John, 122
Wright, Thomas, 143, 146
Wright's Mills, 146

Y

Yegly, Anthony Day, 52
York, J. B., 156
Young Block, 130
Young, Isaac, 67
Youngblood, Richard, 112

Z

Zaizer, Jacob P., 144, 149
Zigler, George, 145

Made in the USA
Middletown, DE
15 March 2022